GUIDE TO DECISION MAKING

OTHER ECONOMIST BOOKS

Guide to Analysing Companies
Guide to Business Modelling
Guide to Business Planning
Guide to Cash Management
Guide to Economic Indicators
Guide to the European Union
Guide to Financial Management
Guide to Financial Markets
Guide to Hedge Funds
Guide to Investment Strategy
Guide to Management Ideas and Gurus
Guide to Managing Growth
Guide to Organisation Design
Guide to Project Management
Guide to Supply Chain Management
Numbers Guide
Style Guide

Book of Business Quotations
Book of Isms
Book of Obituaries
Brands and Branding
Business Consulting
Business Strategy
Buying Professional Services
The City
Coaching and Mentoring
Doing Business in China
Economics
Emerging Markets
Marketing
Megachange
Modern Warfare, Intelligence and Deterrence
Organisation Culture
Successful Strategy Execution
The World of Business

Directors: an A–Z Guide
Economics: an A–Z Guide
Investment: an A–Z Guide
Negotiation: an A–Z Guide

Pocket World in Figures

The
Economist

GUIDE TO DECISION MAKING

MAKING

Getting it more right than wrong

Helga Drummond

WILEY

John Wiley & Sons, Inc.

Published by John Wiley & Sons, Inc., Hoboken, New Jersey.

Published simultaneously in Canada.

Published in Great Britain and the rest of the world by Profile Books Ltd

For general information on our other products and services or for technical
support, please contact our Customer Care Department within the United States
at (800) 762-2974, outside the United States at (317) 572-3993 or fax (317) 572-4002.

Wiley also publishes its books in a variety of electronic formats. Some content
that appears in print may not be available in electronic books. For more
information about Wiley products, visit our web site at www.wiley.com.

Library of Congress Cataloging-in-Publication Data:
ISBN 978-1-118-18535-3 (cloth); ISBN 978-1-118-24055-7 (ebk);
ISBN 978-1-118-26515-4 (ebk); ISBN 978-1-118-22756-5 (ebk)

Printed in the United States of America
10 9 8 7 6 5 4 3 2 1

To Fay Fielding (née Smith)

Contents

Acknowledgements

THERE ARE MANY PEOPLE who in their different ways have helped me in writing this book and who I would like to thank. I am grateful to the provost of Gresham College, Sir Roderick Floud, for the invitation to speak on aspects of what is in the book and to Barbara Anderson for delivering the lecture when a flash flood prevented me from leaving home. Similar thanks are due to Karen Carr, professor of human systems at Cranfield University, for invitations to lecture at the Defence Academy in Shrivenham. Lord Clifton of Rathmore was kind enough to share his observations on the global financial crisis and its aftermath; William Tankard of GFMS, a precious metals consultancy, helped me with information on gold production; Leslie Willcocks, professor of technology work and globalisation at the London School of Economics, provided statistics on re-contracting; and John Gapper was most illuminating on rogue traders.

Colleagues on the Defence Scientific Advisory Council have been a source of inspiration and insight. I particularly thank Sir Peter Knight for his insights into how scientists think, Scott Steadman for informal discussion on what makes a good engineer and allusions to "feeling the metal" that informs part of Chapter 4, and Ian Poll, professor of aerospace engineering at Cranfield University, for his observations on planning. Thanks are also due to Major General Alan Macklin for sharing his insights into the art of management.

Without the influence of Rear-Admiral Trevor Spires this book would have never been started. Once it was, the task of writing has been lightened by conversations away from my desk in places such as Lincoln's Inn, where the delightful Christopher Barnett QC explained the true meaning of patience to me. The Royal Institution of Chartered Surveyors also provided an hospitable home away from the computer, with Alex Baird, Bob Clarke and Violetta Parylo making it particularly so. The farewell dinner at Roux in Parliament Square that they arranged was a supremely handsome gesture. Part of the intellectual backcloth of the book is built on research projects funded by the Economic and Social Research Council, and I warmly acknowledge its support. I owe an intellectual debt to Richard Harvey Brown, a professor at the University of Maryland, who sadly I never met before he died. Thanks are due to Catherine Griffiths of Imperial College London, senior editor of the *Journal of Information Technology*, for her patience and help in developing the ideas on management information systems and risk management that form part of Chapter 4. I am also grateful to Murray Dalziel, professor of management and director of the University of Liverpool Management School, for his support and encouragement. Andrew Derrington, professor of psychology and executive pro-vice-chancellor at the University of Liverpool, held a series of grant-writing workshops that found an unexpected use. Julie Reddy responded with unfailing patience and courtesy to requests for technical help.

Daniel Crewe and Stephen Brough went beyond the normal duties of a commissioning editor in reading draft chapters. Their suggestions have greatly improved the book. Janet Briddon read the manuscript and I am immensely grateful for her work. I would also like to thank Penny Williams for her good-humoured and authoritative copy-editing. Any mistakes are mine. The writing of this book coincided with two bad winters, and the experience made me question my decision to live in a remote 300-year-old farmhouse. I certainly could have done without having to clamber through the woods at six in the morning. The reward was a set of fox prints in the snow – illuminated by moonlight. The day's teaching was delivered in hiking boots. But it was delivered.

I was walking past Temple church in London. From within came the sound of the hymn "Jerusalem" being sung. It was a bitterly cold night. I had had a long day. But I paused. It was as if 40-odd years had not passed, the hymn being a poignant codicil to school days and essays written with a junior cartridge pen. Barbara Windle, former head teacher of the Mount School, York, wrote of the role of the educator:[1]

It demands we see in the failures of adolescence and its many confusions, the possibility of something untangled, clear, directed. It asks us to sustain that faith through a multiplicity of discouraging experiences and indeed to find within those experiences the grounds for hope.

Fay Fielding (née Smith), thank you.

Helga Drummond
May 2012

Introduction

I meditate upon mankind's advancement
From flint sparks into million-volted glare
That shows us everything but the future –
And leaves us not much wiser than we were.

Siegfried Sassoon

WE MAKE OUR DECISIONS. Our decisions make us and our organisations.

In theory, decision-making is simple. A problem emerges. The goal is defined and the possible options for achieving it and solving the problem identified. These options are then analysed and the one that seems most effective is selected. Powerful mathematical tools are available to facilitate the task. Yet if it is so simple, why do businesses keep getting it wrong?

There is no shortage of examples of poor decision-making. Lehman Brothers might have survived if it had raised more capital or merged while it still had the chance. But it left it too late. The Royal Bank of Scotland was almost ruined by the decision to acquire ABN Amro. Toyota's reputation was severely dented by the furore caused by its reluctance to recall vehicles with potentially lethal faults. Porsche lost its independence as a result of a decision to mount a takeover for VW. The Deepwater Horizon disaster exposed flaws in BP's decision-making. Many more failures go unreported. Yet the costs, direct and indirect, are borne by shareholders, employees, taxpayers and ultimately society at large. Those costs, moreover, sometimes involve injury or loss of life.

No organisation makes perfect decisions all the time. Decision-making is a lot harder than the textbooks suggest. All decisions involving uncertainty risk failing. Ultimately, there is nothing for it but for decision-makers to "put up the money and roll the dice". Yet there is no need for firms to learn the hard way. The starting point is to distinguish between a mistake made amid the fog of war and a systematic error of judgment. We can do nothing about the fog of war. But systematic errors are avoidable. This book is about why systematic errors are made, how they result in bad decisions and how to make better decisions.

Predictable surprises

Failure frequently takes firms by surprise. Lehman Brothers was hardly the only firm trading in subprime mortgage derivatives. The Royal Bank of Scotland was not the first firm to pay too much for an acquisition. Toyota may well have been right about the media exaggerating the so-called "sticky pedals" problem. Porsche's bid for VW almost succeeded. BP thought it had instilled a safety culture. The point is that in retrospect, failure often seems to have been virtually inevitable.

Strictly speaking, if something is inevitable it can hardly be a surprise. This book explores that paradox and goes off the beaten track in the process. There are no decision trees, no spreadsheets, no financial tables and no mathematical models in the text. Quantification and analysis have their place. But this book is mainly concerned with what lies behind the mask of science – the gap that may lie between theory and practice, and between what we know and believe to be true and what actually is true.

The main theme of this book is that rationality is not so much a guide as an achievement, forged from myriad non-rational influences. It explores the nature of these influences and how they can influence decisions. For example, in theory firms scan the environment looking for threats and opportunities. In practice it may be more accurate to describe firms as forever creating their environments and editing out the inconvenient elements. By acting as if their creations are real, firms can end up occupying a world of fantasy.

Nothing is certain. Not even the "known knowns". The quotation from Siegfried Sassoon's poem "Cleaning the Candelabrum" reminds us that even the most powerful mathematical models of choice offer no certainty. But if we understand the uncertainty that lies behind them, we can make better decisions.

Where surprises come from

Calamity loves the overconfident. This is because overconfidence tempts us to take bigger and bigger risks. Chapter 1 explains why most decision-makers are overconfident to begin with and why repeated success can amplify the danger. Humility is the cure.

Perception is reality. Yet perception is usually wrong. Chapter 2 explains why. To make sense of their worlds, decision-makers filter information. Filters are double edged. They speed up decision-making by enabling decision-makers to separate the wheat from the chaff. But filters also distort vision. Since those distortions are systematic, provided decision-makers know about them they can correct for them.

Firms use filters too. Chapter 3 explains how and why those filters can prevent firms from seeing the blindingly obvious. Particular attention is paid to why problem formulation is not a neutral (rational) exercise but open to all manner of influences and why "reality" is best viewed as a myth. All myths are partly true. Therefore all myths are partly false. The trouble is decision-makers forget about the bit that is false. Instead of defining reality aggressively, decision-makers should treat it as "useful fiction".

In theory, information keeps decision-makers in touch with reality. In practice, it can have the opposite effect. Chapter 4 explains why this is so. More specifically, what tends to happen is that the decision-maker's graphs, spreadsheets and the like become *the* way of seeing when these artefacts are only ever *a* way of seeing. Since a way of seeing is also a way of not seeing, information can lead decision-makers into a hermetically sealed world where everything seems to be under control. But that belief is an illusion. That is why it is important for decision-makers to escape to reality.

Chapter 5 focuses on group dynamics. Groups can make better decisions than individuals acting alone because they bring diverse mindsets and experience to problems. But groups are not only prone to making the same errors of judgment as individuals; they can also become conspiracies of optimism. Many of the problems of group dynamics are hard to eliminate completely. Good leadership is the most important thing.

Chapter 6 is where all the vested interests, truths, half-truths and arguments of the day converge. The starting point of this chapter on politics and political behaviour in firms is why control is never perfect. Not even in the most autocratic firms. The main political tactics that people use to influence decisions are then explored, including the role of "silent power". Politics may give rise to the "four deadly Ds": delay, dissimulation, deflection and dilution. Yet this chapter should not be read as an argument for banning politics. Politics may explain the aphorism that a camel is a horse produced by a committee. But the absence of politics may result in something worse.

Chapter 7 explores the "irrationality of rationality". It takes issue with rationality itself. The main idea is that decision-makers can act in ways that are logical and purposeful, yet the results are self-defeating. An important lesson is that "more" of a good thing is not always better.

Robert Burns, a poet, reminds us in his poem *To a Mouse* that the best-laid plans frequently go awry. Yet we know a lot more about how to get firms moving than how to stop them when decisions threaten to go awry. Chapter 8 focuses on escalation of commitment. It explores why, instead of culling poor projects, decision-makers may reinvest in them, only to end up "throwing good money after bad". Good management is the answer.

Chapter 9 considers a more insidious form of "lock-in" known as entrapment. Whereas escalation results from deliberate decisions to reinvest in failing projects, entrapment happens mainly through the simple passage of time. Even so, entrapment may be avoidable, provided decision-makers remember three things: the passage of time may not be without cost; doing nothing is itself a decision – with consequences; more may be lost by not taking a risk.

Chapter 10 deals with options. These are presented as a style of thinking. That thinking can be applied to minimise escalation and entrapment and even profit from uncertainty. The main types of option are discussed as well as some of the pitfalls.

The last chapter discusses controversial research that suggests that the most important thing in decision-making is to do what feels right. When the time comes to "put up the money and roll the dice", what should have the last word, intuition or analysis?

Illusions of control: the confidence trap

I

"Think it possible that you may be mistaken."
Quaker Advices and Queries

IN OCTOBER 2008, Wendelin Wiedeking, Porsche's chief executive, announced an imminent takeover of VW. Hedge funds that had bet on VW's share price falling were confounded. Tearful fund managers confronted huge losses. Yet within six months, Porsche was almost bankrupt. In a humiliating reversal, VW turned the tables on the predatory Porsche, which lost its independence – when it had seemed to come within an ace of success. Porsche was ruined by overconfidence. Yet why was Porsche so sure? What made it believe that it could dominate a company 82 times its size?

Calamity loves overconfidence. This chapter explores what causes overconfidence and how it can lead to calamity. The starting point is that most managers are confident to begin with. Repeated success makes them even more confident and therefore more prone to behaving recklessly – though without realising it. Business is a game of skill and luck. The important thing is not to depend too much on luck.

Illusions of control

In 1980, Shelly Taylor, a psychologist, published a controversial book entitled *Positive Illusions*.[1] Taylor's theme (supported by substantial research evidence) is that most people are out of touch with reality most of the time. For instance, whereas depression is popularly regarded as seeing things as worse than they are, Taylor argues that depression is seeing things as they are.

Psychologists call it the illusion of control, a reference to our innate tendency as human beings to overestimate our ability to achieve outcomes, even those that are obviously due to chance. For instance, would you prefer to choose a lottery ticket or accept a ticket from the shopkeeper? (Assume that the shopkeeper is honest.) Logically, it makes no difference to the probability of winning. Yet you may prefer to choose the ticket – why?

Research into gambling behaviour has shown that players often behave as if they can control chance events. For instance, they shake the cup hard if they need high numbers on the dice and softly if they need low numbers. Then there is the daily "to do" list. Those who compile such lists typically overestimate what they can achieve in a day. Yet that does not stop them from compiling yet another list – as if they never learn. Overconfidence may also encourage frequent trading in stockmarkets. That is, frequent traders may assume that their stock selections will be so successful that transaction costs will prove immaterial.

Our innate tendency to overestimate our abilities means we often see ourselves as superior to other people. We also view ourselves more positively than others see us. We often overstate the value of our own contributions, while undervaluing contributions made by other people. For instance, in 1923 two Canadian scientists, Frederick Banting and James Macleod, won the Nobel Prize in medicine for the discovery of insulin. Banting claimed that Macleod had been more of a hindrance than a help while Macleod omitted Banting's name from all the speeches describing the research leading up to the discovery. Similarly, in group work, most people remember their own contributions rather than those made by other members of the group. Negotiators often underestimate the bargaining power of their opponents and overestimate the likelihood that their final offer will be accepted.

Research has shown that most people value themselves too highly. The result may be that they price themselves (or their firms) out of the market. The chief executive of a multinational company says:

We needed a piece of research done. Firms in the US and Australia wanted around $20 million for the job. A firm in India said they would do it if we re-kitted their laboratories – $3 million – and they *had all the infrastructure and staff in place to support the research – same as the US and Australia.*

Lesson: be humble.

Overconfidence breeds complacency. When NASA first launched the Apollo moon-landing expeditions in the 1960s, it was so afraid of failure that engineers had to prove that every launch was safe before it could go ahead. As the technology became routine, the system developed a false confidence in itself. Safety standards were lowered. That meant rockets would be launched unless engineers could prove that it was unsafe to do so. The consequences of NASA's complacency were graphically demonstrated when the spaceship *Challenger* exploded on take-off killing all on board – before a television audience of millions. Similarly, as memories of Three Mile Island and Chernobyl receded, attitudes towards nuclear energy relaxed. Then in 2011 an earthquake struck Japan followed by a tsunami. Reactors melted down releasing high levels of radioactivity into the atmosphere and the ocean. The disaster also exposed systemic weaknesses, including poor location of the reactors, poor accident preparation, poor emergency response and weak regulation. It was the old story. We forget that a history of no accidents does not mean something is safe.

Toyota's leaders inflicted huge damage upon the company by refusing to recall vehicles with potentially lethal accelerator pedals. Toyota had known about the "sticky accelerator pedal" problem for months (possibly years) before reports began appearing in the news in late 2009, but acted only when forced to do so by mounting public pressure. The company was finally galvanised into action following worldwide dissemination of a recording of the last words of a passenger in a hired Lexus that allegedly sped out of control. In a 911 emergency call made just before the car crashed, Chris Lastrella is heard saying, "We're in a Lexus ... and we're going north on 125 and our accelerator is stuck ... we're in trouble ... there's no brakes ... we're approaching the intersection ... hold on ... hold on and pray ... pray."[2] Lastrella was killed in the crash along with the driver of the car and two other passengers. Part of Toyota's problem may have been that it simply could not believe that its cars could be less than perfect.

The confidence trap

Nothing succeeds like success, according to the proverb. Yet repeated success can destroy us. This is because, if we are consistently successful, we expect to succeed. Just as people who experience early wins in games of chance tend to raise their bets, repeated success can tempt us to take bigger and bigger risks because we feel invulnerable. Barings almost came to grief 100 years before it was destroyed by Nick Leeson's activities in the early 1990s. During the 1880s Barings was flying high as evidenced by the runaway success of the Guinness flotation of 1886, when investors, desperate to acquire shares, resorted to wrapping their application forms round stones and hurling them through Barings' windows. Barings then determined upon an even bolder venture, namely a waterworks project in Argentina. This time Lord Revelstoke, Barings' senior partner, decided that underwriting was superfluous. The issue failed. Barings was left holding the shares. The firm had to be rescued by the government because of the systemic threat. The partners lost everything. Lord Revelstoke's mistake was dispensing with underwriting. That decision made the venture much more risky. Lord Revelstoke took the decision because he assumed that the Guinness success would be repeated. Such was his overconfidence that it never occurred to him that it might not be.

Modern firms are by no means immune from the overconfidence trap. In 2007, Vodafone triumphantly launched a $10.9 billion expansion into India by acquiring a 66% stake in Hutchinson Essar, renamed Vodafone Essar. Vodafone expected to acquire a substantial share of India's growing market for mobile telephony. Yet within three years, it was forced to write down the value of its Indian business by 25%. This embarrassing reversal happened because whereas most countries have three or four network operators, India has 15. An overly confident Vodafone failed adequately to consider the implications of this basic statistic. (The venture has since prospered despite the inauspicious start.) Similarly, Porsche's status as the most profitable carmaker in the world may have gone to its directors' heads. Success also boosts our self-esteem. High self-esteem may also explain (but not excuse) unethical behaviour. That is, executives with high self-esteem may believe that they are incapable of acting unethically.

Success and luck: the deadly cocktail

Success in business requires skill and luck. Strategy matters, but so too does the roll of the dice. In July 2008, a luxury hotel, the Yang Sing Oriental, adjacent to Manchester's well-known Yang Sing restaurant, opened to considerable fanfare. Designed to attract so-called "high rollers" willing and able to pay over £300 a night for a room, the £8m venture lasted just eight months before being forced to close; the building was eventually sold to a property developer. The timing was certainly unlucky, as the hotel opened only weeks before the start of the global financial crisis. Yet was there ever a market to begin with?

We will probably never know. Although it can be difficult to accurately pinpoint how far outcomes reflect skill, and how much is owed to chance, decision-makers seldom entertain doubt. We almost invariably attribute success to our innate abilities and failure to bad luck or other people's shortcomings.

We are also biased in how we remember. That is, we tend to rewrite history, casting ourselves in a favourable light. Moreover, we are likely to believe in our own view of events, even though it is not borne out by the facts. For instance, when investors are asked to recall how their stock selections performed, their answers may bear little resemblance to the actual performance of those investments. Almost invariably, investors inflated performance in their own minds. Similarly, executives are likely to remember past ventures as more successful than they really were, and to glorify their own role in promoting those ventures. Such self-serving beliefs may preserve egos, but they block learning.

Bunker mentality

Bunker mentality is the ultimate overconfidence trap. As the Allied armies advanced upon Berlin in the early months of 1945, Hitler retreated into a deep concrete bunker, seldom emerging into the bomb-blasted city. Cut off from the outside world, he became hopelessly unrealistic, moving armies that no longer existed and directing an air force that had long since been obliterated. Bunker mentality refers to decision-makers who cut themselves off and, as a result, lose touch with reality.

When reality is removed from the equation, anything seems possible. As Lehman Brothers' financial position worsened, Dick Fuld, the chief executive, became increasingly remote and stopped visiting trading floors. During the weekend of September 13th-14th 2008, as the American banking elite met to discuss what to do about Lehman's impending collapse, Fuld waited in his office, expecting to negotiate terms, not realising that his authority had melted away.

Bunker mentality is a flight to psychological safety. It can take various forms, for example managers sheltering behind computer screens or perpetually travelling, or leaders becoming almost invisible during a crisis. When Siemens came under pressure from shareholders after management took a 30% pay rise, the then chief executive, Klaus Kleinfield, was criticised for keeping a low profile. Indeed, bunker mentality may explain why Siemens was insensitive to shareholders' feelings in the first place. More specifically, shareholders were already angry because of the decision to pay $300m to BenQ, a consumer electronics company, to relieve Siemens of its mobile-phone business. Within a year BenQ had gone bankrupt. There was also an alleged $556m bribery scandal. Siemens's leaders may have become so remote from reality that they failed to recognise how their decisions might be seen by those outside the bunker.

Avoiding the overconfidence trap

The clearest sign of overconfidence is when decision-makers do not stop to think that they could be wrong. Indeed, Porsche had every reason to expect that the Volkswagen Law (see box on page 12) would be changed, not least because the EU had long opposed it. Yet nothing is certain except that hubris will be punished. As the proverb states, there may be many a slip twixt the cup and the lip. Porsche's mistake was to underestimate the determination of local politicians to keep their arcane law. Christian Wulff, premier of Lower Saxony, successfully lobbied Angela Merkel, the German chancellor. With her agreement, the EU's objections were met with only a token revision of the law. The main barrier to Porsche's ambition did not fall after all. Because it was so sure, Porsche had no contingency plans to deal with this eventuality.

Similarly, what may have hurt the hedge fund managers who bet against VW most was discovering that their cleverness had failed them. They were sure that VW's share price would fall. But they discovered that the world was not as predictable as they had thought. Wherever there is uncertainty, failure is a possibility. Decision-makers should never assume success is guaranteed, even though the odds are good.

If something seems rock-solid certain, apply the Quaker advice "think it possible that you may be mistaken".[3] In other words, do not allow the strength of your convictions to propel you towards disaster. For example, even if the sticky-pedal problem was exaggerated, Toyota urgently needed to address the issue of public confidence. Similarly, Porsche should have posed the question, "what if" the Volkswagen Law is not repealed? Then subtract unnecessary risk. The greater the risk being run, the more success depends on luck. Sooner or later, luck must fail.

Another technique for exposing overconfidence is to invoke experience. Economics holds that making an economically rational decision involves computing the expected value of an event and multiplying it by the probability of that event occurring. Both computations are ultimately guesses and therefore open to all manner of influences including over-optimism. Do those computations square with actual experience? Management by walking round is a simple but effective cure for bunker mentality. To be more precise, walking round, asking questions and listening to the answers; and seeking the views of objective outsiders where necessary.

The trouble is that overconfidence can tempt decision-makers to disregard the self-discipline that made them successful in the first place. Porsche owed much of its success to following an evolutionary strategy, not venturing too far, too fast from the core business of making sports cars and not making too many changes to models all at once. Yet the caution that had served Porsche so well was abandoned when it came to the VW venture. Sun Tzu, an ancient Chinese military philosopher, counsels commanders to be as careful in victory as in defeat. It is good advice for business.

David versus Goliath: Porsche and VW

Porsche was founded by Ferdinand Porsche in 1931, based in Stuttgart, Germany. Originally the firm did not make cars itself but sold consultancy to other manufacturers. This included a commission to contribute to the development of the original Volkswagen Beetle.

Porsche still sells consultancy – clients include Audi, Seat and Subaru – but the company is now best known for its sports cars, notably the Porsche 911. Employing only around 2,000 staff, turning out 100,000 cars a year, Porsche has retained most of its production in Germany, unlike many other car manufacturers who have outsourced production to low-cost countries. During the 1990s Porsche almost went bankrupt, but otherwise has been extremely profitable. Moreover, unlike other luxury carmakers such as Aston Martin, owned by Ford, and Maserati, owned by Fiat, Porsche remained independent.

So it might have continued. Except that in late 2005, Wendelin Wiedeking, then chief executive, decided that Porsche would build a stake in VW, a company 82 times bigger than itself. Porsche sold 100,000 cars a year, VW sold 6m. Over the next three years, Porsche purchased options to buy VW shares and made about as much from dealing in these financial contracts as from making cars. But that was only on paper. In 2008, moreover, it revealed that it had used a special type of option that did not have to be disclosed and that involved hedging against a rising VW share price.

Risk as choice

Above all it is important to be mindful of what risk means. Although the dictionary defines risk as "mischance", "hazard" and "possibility of bad consequences", the word actually derives from the early Italian *risicare*, meaning "to dare". This portrays risk as a choice rather than a fate. Lord Revelstoke could have reduced the risk involved in the Argentinian project by arranging underwriting. He chose not to. Porsche chose to take on a much, much bigger company and to

VW's share price quadrupled when it was announced that Porsche had acquired a 75% stake in the company. Consequently, many hedge funds that had bet on VW's share price falling incurred heavy losses.

Porsche took two big risks. First, it borrowed around €10 billion in order to increase its stake in VW from just under 51% to 75%. Second, it relied upon the repeal of the so-called Volkswagen Law, a local law restricting individuals to 20% of the voting rights in VW, regardless of the size of their holdings, and giving the state of Lower Saxony a veto on major decisions. As the European Commission had long been opposed to this law, Porsche had good reason to believe that it would be repealed. If it were not, Porsche could not assume control of VW and its shareholding would be useless.

Both gambles failed. When the global financial crisis struck, Porsche's sales fell and the company ran short of cash to pay interest on debts. Simultaneously, the supply of credit dried up. Indeed, Porsche was allowed to roll over its existing loan only by pledging shares in VW as collateral, and promising to repay over €3m within six months. Worse still, the Volkswagen Law was not repealed. Consequently, Porsche was unable to use its 75% stake in VW to take control of VW's billions of euros, leaving Porsche perilously exposed. The result was a forced merger with VW.

rely upon the government to repeal a law it had never said it would repeal. Toyota chose to ignore mounting criticism. In other words, calamity does not just strike. Firms bring it upon themselves through the choices they make.

2 Blinkered vision: the judgment trap

"He who sees what is now has seen all things."

Marcus Aurelius

ON THURSDAY FEBRUARY 23RD 1995 the directors of Barings Bank hosted a lunch for financial movers and shakers in the City of London. The conversation was animated, much of it focusing on a new venture in Mexico. The directors had "no idea", a guest said afterwards, that Barings, one of the oldest and most respected banks in the City, was about to collapse. Yet for weeks markets in East Asia had been ablaze with rumours about Barings incurring massive exposure to a mystery client who might default. Why did it not see the danger signals until it was too late?

To make sense of a decision-making environment it is necessary to simplify. Simplification means filtering out irrelevant data. Filters are double edged. They speed up the task of decision-making. But they can create a false sense of certainty by distorting what decision-makers see, and how they see. This chapter explains the main judgmental traps and how decision-makers can avoid them.[1] The main thing to be aware of is that the distortions are systematic. Therefore decision-makers can correct for them.

Look no further: confirmation traps

The confirmation trap refers to our innate tendency to pay more attention to information that supports our preconceived ideas, and to downplay or even dismiss contradictory information. We tend to accept information that confirms our beliefs uncritically, whereas if the information contradicts those beliefs, our reaction is likely to be: "Must I believe it?"

Seven traps for the unwary

1 Confirmation – seeing what we want to see
2 Anchoring – using irrelevant information
3 Analogy – missing important differences
4 Availability – overuse of most recent or easily obtainable information
5 Vividness – being seduced by alluring images and glittering opportunities
6 Instant response – decisions based on emotion, not reason
7 Expectation – seeing what we expect to see

Barings might have been saved, albeit severely damaged, if it had investigated the rumours circulating in financial markets in East Asia, particularly when respected banks like Flemings, Goldman Sachs and Morgan Stanley began warning their clients to be careful about using Barings as a counterparty. Instead, it succumbed to the confirmation trap. That is, it assumed that the market was finding it hard to accept that such a small merchant bank could perform so magnificently. It never occurred to Barings that the rumours about its fallibility might be true.

Why first impressions matter: anchoring traps

Before reading this section, jot down the last three digits of your home telephone number. Now guess when the Taj Mahal was built. Unless you happen to know the correct answer, it is quite likely that your estimate of the date (high or low number) will be influenced by the previous irrelevant piece of information concerning your telephone number – known as the anchoring trap.[2]

Anchoring means basing a prediction on an initial reference point and then making adjustments. The reference point may be historical data, such as information about past performance, or some other source of information. It may even be completely unrelated to the question, like the last three digits of a telephone number, but it influences the estimate all the same. Moreover, few people adjust sufficiently away from the initial anchoring point. For instance, a surveyor's valuation of a property should be based on expert knowledge. Otherwise, why go to the expense of obtaining a survey? Yet anchoring implies that the valuation is likely to be unduly influenced by the guide price. Anchoring also explains why salary offers are often based upon what candidates are already earning – regardless of whether they might be overpaid or underpaid, and regardless of market rates. Clearly, there are practical considerations as people rarely change jobs for less money. The point is that the salary offer is likely to be influenced by inappropriate anchors. We may think that our judgment is based on objective information and in a sense it is. But it is the wrong information.

Anchoring also explains why first impressions are so important. Interviewers are likely to make a judgment during the first three minutes but then fail to adjust it as the interview progresses and new information emerges. Confirmation biases may also come in to play as decision-makers spend much of the interview unconsciously searching for information to support their initial judgment. This is why no one gets a second chance to make a first impression.

Another important effect of anchoring is that we expect past performance to be repeated. For instance, if we have a good meal in a restaurant, we expect the same level of experience next time we visit because of that initial anchoring. Likewise, firms may instruct law firms because of their track record with similar cases, expecting them to repeat previous success. Yet probabilities seldom remain constant. Past performance may not be sustained because of the shifting tides of organisation, as people, hardware and systems change.

Seen it all before: analogy traps

The analogy trap means judging one thing by its resemblance to another. Analogy can be efficient use of brainpower because it enables decision-makers to apply tried and tested solutions to problems that are specifically different but generically similar. In other words, analogy can save decision-makers from reinventing the wheel.

The danger is that decision-makers may miss important differences between past and present cases. New chief executives may be slow to recognise that a style of management that suited their old organisation does not work in the new one. Monsanto diversified into biotechnology because it seemed to complement its existing chemicals business. It found that although there were similarities between the two businesses, there was one crucial difference it had not recognised. Chemical research is a mature field. Discoveries need strong market applications. In contrast, biotechnology requires basic research organised centrally to promulgate discoveries. The two proved incompatible. So Monsanto decided to spin off its chemical business. Had it recognised the problem before committing itself, it might have taken a different approach. Similarly, when a cloud of volcanic ash halted flights in and out of the UK and elsewhere in April 2010, some airlines wasted resources and added to the suffering of passengers by implementing business-continuity plans that broke down because they were not designed for such prolonged and widespread disruption. The airlines saw the similarities between past and present disruptions but not the differences.

Another manifestation of the analogy trap is that we may base our estimates of success on the similarity of a venture to previous ventures. For instance, it is thought that venture capitalists are more likely to support an entrepreneur if the person reminds them of someone they have worked with successfully in the past. Similarly, interviewers may be attracted to candidates with similar profiles to themselves. By allowing themselves to be influenced by superficial similarities, decision-makers can end up supporting bad ideas and poor job candidates and rejecting good ones. Another word for this is stereotyping, or fixed images – for example, the types of cars that allegedly appeal to hairdressers or boy racers, and the characteristics of rogue traders. Stereotyping happens a lot in recruitment. Firms tend to opt for people who match a given set of criteria rather than those who might be good at doing a particular job in a particular context. Firms such as Facebook try to avoid this problem by recruiting people for their potential. Less enlightened employers who recruit solely on experience and qualifications are more likely to end up with "square pegs" in "round holes".

The analogy trap can mean that experience works against us.

"The last thing we expected": the collapse of Barings Bank

Nick Leeson joined Barings in 1989 as a back-office clerk based in London. In March 1992 he was seconded to Singapore to run the back office, which is where trades are settled and associated paperwork processed. He was then given front-office trading responsibilities while also retaining overall supervision responsibility for the back office. In investment banking, trading and responsibility for processing the subsequent paperwork (known as settlements) are normally segregated to prevent fraud – Leeson's roles were completely unsegregated. In the noise and clamour of trading pits, he made a lot of mistakes learning how to execute business and, as a result, lost money. When those losses became too big to hide, he tried to recoup them by secretly selling options.

As a result of his unauthorised options trading, Leeson lost even more money. But because the premium he gained for granting options was booked as pure profit, he appeared to be highly successful. By January 1995, his losses had reached about £200m – almost half of Barings' entire capital. During the next seven weeks or so, that sum rose exponentially as Leeson redoubled his bets. Consequently, by late January his profits appeared to outstrip those of the entire organisation.

Yet signs of malfeasance had long been evident. A few months after Leeson arrived in Singapore, Barings noticed that it seemed to have paid out £10m more than it had collected from Leeson's customers. An investigation proved inconclusive, so the unreconciled amounts were vaguely attributed to the different time zones. Over the next three years that figure inexplicably

Intuitively, we might think that doctors become more competent with age – at least up to a point. But diagnostic accuracy deteriorates over time. Firefighters are most likely to be killed not when they are new to the job, but when they have been in it for about ten years and think rose to over £100m. Moreover, every day Leeson was faxing requests for millions of pounds in collateral (margin) to support his unauthorised trading. Yet he was invariably evasive about why he needed so much money and he always made sure that the back-office paperwork made everything reconcile. Treasury staff in London knew that Leeson was making up the figures because they were too neat. For example, some days Leeson said the split between client and house positions was 60/40; the next day he simply reversed the ratio. In January 1995, Coopers & Lybrand discovered an apparent £50m irregular trade in Leeson's accounts. He claimed that it was an "over-the-counter" transaction and that he had forgotten to collect the money. By now his margin calls were straining Barings' resources so he was instructed to reduce his positions. But trade went on rising.

During January the rumours about Barings' mystery client grew louder. By mid-February, there was an even more ominous development as respected banks like Goldman Sachs and Morgan Stanley were warning their customers to be careful about dealing with Barings.

A subsequent enquiry by the Bank of England concluded that while each of these warning signs might not have meant much in isolation, taken together they should have sounded the alarm. Yet Barings missed every one until it was too late to save the bank. It was only after Leeson mysteriously disappeared that Barings discovered that the mystery customer was none other than the bank itself.[3]

they have seen it all before.[4] The same applies to business decisions. For example, firms should not assume that all mergers are the same. If they do, they may overlook nuanced differences between previously successful integrations and the challenges posed by a new one.

Misplaced analogy partly explains Barings' demise. Leeson claimed that his unusual profits were derived from arbitrage, buying a quantity in Singapore and immediately selling it on in Osaka and profiting from the price difference between the two markets. That explanation was implausible because price differentials in financial markets are wafer thin and highly unstable. Consequently, there is every risk that prices will move while contracts are executed, resulting in a loss. Barings took Leeson at his word because it had seen it before in the early 1980s, when Barings profited hugely from early entry into emerging markets including Japanese warrants. Barings' chairman, Peter Baring, said:[5]

> We had a number of businesses that were low risk and relatively high profitability; the most pronounced example of this was the Japanese warrant trading business … What none of us believed was that this business would last. The basic instinct … that there is something about this business that defied gravity is something which we shared; but it was in terms of its durability … In our experience, these businesses could last for a period but then they would go. That would happen to us again and again.

A crucial difference between past and present was that in the early 1980s Barings enjoyed a monopoly. By 1995 competitors had long since moved in. Leeson had apparently been arbitraging for nearly three years. If there was so much easy money to be made, why had other banks like Morgan Stanley and Schroders not attempted to move in? It was a question that Barings did not stop to ask. It simply assumed that history was repeating itself.

An analogy may carry no more truth than a superstition. In superstition there is no logical connection between actions and the desired outcome. For example, someone wearing the same socks they wore last time they successfully negotiated a contract expecting repeated success. Top-class riders and athletes rely on relentless preparation, not superstition. It is a good maxim for business.

Out of sight, out of mind: availability traps

Recent events have more impact on decisions than distant ones because of the ease of recall – a phenomenon known as the availability trap. Availability explains why advertisers spend millions of dollars bombarding audiences with messages that their soap powder washes whiter than other soap powders. The aim is to ensure that their brand springs to mind whenever consumers shop for washing powder. Similarly, managers are more likely to choose suppliers whose names come readily to mind, regardless of cost and quality. Availability also means that when managers conduct annual performance appraisals, most of the interview is likely to focus on the last three months.

Alluring images: vividness traps

The chief safety officer of a chemical plant received a visit from the security services. The purpose of the visit was to review security against the risk of possible terrorist attacks. The visit occupied a whole afternoon. Next day, the chief safety officer was asked what the visitors looked like. He replied, "I don't remember."

Vividness refers to our innate tendency to notice bright, alluring images. The visitors probably dressed in dark colours, becoming inconspicuous and unmemorable. Vividness can be a judgmental trap because vivid images deflect attention from statistics. For instance, most business travellers worry more about flying than driving a car, although statistically air travel is much safer than road travel. This is because plane crashes make headline news whereas all but a few car crashes get no or little media coverage.

Vividness can be a trap because if, say, a sales presentation is sufficiently enticing, decision-makers may ignore facts and figures altogether. This is seldom wise because statistical data may give a much more realistic picture of the prospect of success. For instance, John DeLorean persuaded the Northern Ireland Development Agency to invest over £100m (1980 figures) in his motor company through glossy presentations depicting the sports-car dream. The decision-makers ignored industry intelligence that clearly pointed to poor prospects. Within less than two years, the dream factory went bankrupt. Incidentally, one of DeLorean's mistakes was drawing too heavily on his hugely successful experiences at GM. He assumed his new factory was good for 30,000 cars a year. This assumption might have held for a mature production line turning out utility motors. But for a start-up venture producing novel designs, it proved wide of the mark. Moreover, DeLorean ignored an independent marketing report that suggested he would be unlikely to sell more than about 4,000 cars a year.

Vivid events also seem bigger, more frequent and more probable than they really are. For example, when scanning a crowd, a buyer for a fashion house is more likely to notice people wearing bright colours like red and yellow than the majority who happen to be wearing dark colours like black and blue. If the buyer concludes that bright colours are in vogue and stocks up accordingly, the result may be an expensive mistake. Similarly, DeLorean's success at GM may have made him overconfident and therefore careless about using the analogy. No law prevents decision-makers from succumbing to more than one judgmental trap.

Vivid images are also easier to recall than more pallid information. The result can be a form of availability trap. Information that is uppermost in our minds generally has more impact on decisions than information that is submerged, so we may choose a supplier just because the name is familiar – even if it is familiar for negative reasons. This is why bad publicity can be better than no publicity at all.

Conversely, decision-makers may refuse to take a threat seriously unless it is portrayed vividly. For instance, before the terrorist attacks of September 11th 2001 only a minority of Americans thought airport security was important. The attacks also gave huge impetus to business-continuity planning. Scientists have recently discovered a new, drug-resistant, potentially lethal strain of salmonella that hides in people suffering from AIDS. The discovery has received little publicity as cases are confined to Africa. Again, it is unlikely that anyone will worry much about this potentially ominous discovery unless there is a wake-up call. Only a vivid event may convince decision-makers that something is broken.

Too good to lose?

A special form of vividness trap is when an opportunity arises that seems too good to lose. Decision-makers may seize the chance without properly considering the risks and practicalities. For example, a brewery employed just 35 people and produced small quantities of beer. Demand for good-quality beer was growing and the firm's managers were considering how best to exploit the possibilities when they were offered the chance to acquire a redundant brewery. The putative acquisition seemed like a tremendous opportunity because it offered an eightfold increase in capacity for much less money than the other option of doubling on-site capacity. The managers went ahead with the acquisition even though a non-executive director resigned over the decision.

The venture failed. The boiler and lifting gear proved unreliable and the effluent treatment plant became inadequate when the government introduced tighter laws. More importantly, in large-scale production the cash inflows were slower and the margins thinner than the managers were used to with a smaller, more tightly controlled operation. The result was a cash flow crisis followed by a forced merger. A decision-maker said afterwards:[6]

> Really, we seized an opportunity rather than made a planned decision ... we felt we could hardly turn it [the purchase of the brewery] down. We were planning to spend £150,000 expanding our own brewery and the acquisition cost only £115,000.

The brewery's directors thought they were making a good decision, as the economic case for buying the bigger brewery seemed unassailable. Yet that judgment was based on superficial analysis – a vividness trap. The directors also thought they knew the industry. Yet they ignored important differences between the two operations. Both brewed beer but that was where the comparison ended. The directors saw "more of the same" when the two operations were fundamentally different – an analogy trap.

Similarly, during the weekend of September 13th–14th 2008, Barclays Bank tried to buy the whole of Lehman Brothers. It was a tantalising prospect offering instant growth. Bob Diamond, at the time chief executive of Barclays Capital, was reported to have been extremely frustrated when UK regulators stopped the deal. As Andrew Sorkin says in his book *Too Big to Fail*:[7] "How could they have led him so far only to quash the plan at the last moment?" Yet the regulators probably did Barclays a favour, otherwise it might well have ended up with some of Lehman's toxic assets. Moral: all that glitters is not gold.

Emotional rollercoaster: instant-response traps

The instant-response trap refers to decisions made on the spur of the moment, based purely on emotional reaction. The results of such hasty decision-making may not be happy because mood affects our ability to exercise objective judgment. More specifically, extremes of mood (dejection or elation) can amplify the effects of overconfidence or undermine judgment in other ways. For instance, if decision-makers have been grappling with a difficult and important problem for a long time, they may settle for a poor solution just to end the pain of indecision. Sadness is not the same as depression. Sadness arises from thinking of the self. Sad people are particularly susceptible to the influence of anchoring. Anger can blind us to our interests so we end up behaving destructively. To be more precise, psychologists believe that anger makes us feel overconfident because it results in heightened feelings of power and diminished sensitivity to risk.

Conversely, fear and anxiety can make decision-makers more risk averse. Anxiety can also make them more prone to escalation (see Chapter 8). Depression is synonymous with inactivity. Depressed individuals may thus be incapable of taking decisive action when the situation requires it. Being in a good mood can pose problems too. When the sun shines, financial markets rise because good moods lead to over-optimism and make us more likely to take mental shortcuts and invoke stereotypes.

Two dead fish: expectation traps

On Friday July 5th 1991 at one o'clock in the afternoon UK time, regulators suddenly closed down the Bank of Credit and Commerce International (BCCI), an organisation nicknamed the Bank of Crooks and Cocaine International. Accounts involving assets of $20 billion

(1991 figures) in no fewer than 69 countries were immediately frozen. It subsequently emerged that the bank had lived up to its nickname. For instance, the *Financial Times* described BCCI as "a giant hall of mirrors; money that didn't exist, customers who didn't exist, money that went round in circles, money that vanished, and money that popped up out of nowhere".[8]

A question mark had hung over BCCI almost from the start of its 19-year history. In 1980 the Bank of England declined to grant it a full UK banking licence because of its dubious credentials. In 1985 BCCI's auditors discovered that the bank was using questionable accounting methods to disguise losses, but imputed incompetence rather than misfeasance. By 1990 bankers knew that BCCI could hardly raise loans in the main money market because of its association with drug dealing and money-laundering. In January 1991, the auditors discovered that important information on bad loans was missing from BCCI's accounts. Furthermore, loans involving hundreds of millions of pounds were being "parked" with other banks to conceal their existence. Then, in April 1991, a former BCCI employee, Masihur Rahman, told the Bank of England about false accounts and some $300m being diverted through shell companies – money that subsequently vanished.

Yet another three months passed before the regulators acted. Why, demanded the media, did the Bank of England not intervene sooner? Robin Leigh-Pemberton, then governor of the Bank of England, said afterwards: "If we closed down a bank every time we found an instance of fraud, we would have rather fewer banks than we do at the moment."

Indeed, Rahman had been sacked so he had a grievance against BCCI. How seriously should his allegations be taken? An official said: "It was like seeing two dead fish floating down a river ... You did not know how serious a problem you were looking at."

Expectations are reality

Until decision-makers can make sense of a problem, they cannot make a sensible decision. As the story of BCCI shows, that may not be easy, as problems may not emerge full-blown and decision-makers may struggle to distinguish between signal and noise. Yet decision-makers can miss signals that are loud and clear. The official inquiry into the Bank of England's role in supervising BCCI concluded that lots of "dead fish" presented themselves. For instance, in December 1985, an anonymous, poorly typed letter arrived from the Middle East. Signed "Shareholder", it said that 70% of BCCI shareholders were nominees and that there were bad loans totalling 15–20% of BCCI's portfolio. It also called for the "speculative mysterious profitability" of BCCI to be investigated.

Although the Bank of England subsequently described the letter as "of apparent significance with the benefit of hindsight", no effective investigation was ever made. Nor were similarly disquieting reports and rumours probed. Why were the signals missed?

Expectations dictate what we see and hear. For instance, a tired airline pilot is running out of flying hours, the control tower is busy and visibility is poor. The pilot is expecting to hear, "OK take-off", when the air-traffic controller actually says "OK stand by for take-off". Likewise, the air-traffic controller hears the reply as, "We are at take-off position", when the pilot actually says, "We are taking off". It is a recipe for disaster. Similarly, the failure of the American authorities to anticipate the terrorist attacks of September 11th 2001 reflects a failure of expectations. Aviation security experts did not expect that an aircraft would ever be used as a weapon, even though truck bombs and attacks launched from boats (such as the bombing of the USS Cole in October 2000) foreshadowed that possibility. So although the authorities knew that "something bad was up", they could not see how to connect the pieces of the jigsaw – even though those pieces included reports about individuals paying cash for flying lessons who were not interested in learning how to take off or land planes. Putting those pieces together to form a coherent picture required a leap of imagination that transcended official expectations. According to The 9/11 Commission Report, "No one looked at the bigger picture; no analytic work foresaw the lightning that could connect the thundercloud to the ground." Expectations, that is, our theories of the world, dictate what counts as data and what data counts.

Expectations are powerful realities. Once we formulate an explanation for something, rather than adjust our explanation as new information emerges, we rationalise the new information to fit the existing explanation. The cure for this problem is that the definition of a situation must fit all observed events, however bizarre these events may seem. For example, Kweku Adoboli, a trader who was accused of fraud for allegedly hiding losses of $2.3 billion on UBS's Delta One equity derivatives desk, was investigated not as a result of action by compliance officers or an internal audit, but because a security guard began to wonder why Adoboli habitually turned up for work at two o'clock in the morning. The point is that the more bizarre the observed event, the more important it is to account for it. Yet the temptation is to dismiss it, precisely because it makes no sense.

Moreover, once we formulate an explanation for something, incredible blind spots for information to the contrary can develop. For example, staff in Barings' treasury department knew that Leeson's figures were too neat to be true. They assumed he was so busy exploiting a bubble of profit that he was letting administration slip and making up the numbers so that they tallied – as indeed he was. Barings knew Leeson's roles were completely unsegregated. No wonder he was forgetting things when he was trying to do two jobs. And regarding the mystery customer, Barings assumed that since Leeson's positions were matched (contract to buy matched with an equal and opposite contract to sell), and since Osaka published trading positions and the Singapore International Monetary Exchange (Simex) did not, the market was seeing only half of the equation. In fact, as Barings could have discovered, Leeson's positions were completely open.

Another impediment to sense-making was the sheer scale of Leeson's activities. When we encounter something that is so outlandish and so far beyond the realm of experience that it seems incredible, we may simply refuse to believe it, saying to ourselves, "It can't be, therefore it isn't." If Leeson's accounts had been £10,000 or £100,000 adrift, instead of £100m, Barings might have been suspicious. We cannot conceive what we cannot imagine.

Imagination may be constrained by experience. Banks may contain rotten apples, but BCCI's supervisor might have found it hard to imagine that the whole barrel was rotten. Likewise, Bernard Madoff's US-based hedge fund (a $65 billion fraud) came to regulators' attention long before the scam was exposed in 2008. Since 1992, there had been repeated complaints to the Securities and Exchange Commission (SEC) pointing out that Madoff's consistently high returns were hugely improbable, particularly given his primitive trading strategy and his claim to possess unerring intuition. Even more tellingly, complainants pointed out that there was no trace of any counterparties to Madoff's alleged trades. If his fund were genuine, by definition, no counterparty would be willing to trade because they would always lose. Yet every investigation by the SEC exonerated Madoff. The fraud came to light only when the global financial crisis prompted large numbers of investors to withdraw funds and those withdrawals could not be paid from receipts from new investors. Madoff confessed, not to the SEC but to his family. For years evidence had been staring the regulators in the face. They may have missed it because a $65 billion Ponzi scheme was inconceivable, and the idea that a man of such standing as Madoff (he had been non-executive chairman of the NASDAQ stockmarket and was highly respected in investment circles) could be involved in such a scheme was also inconceivable. Faced with the seemingly inconceivable, people may hesitate to report their suspicions for fear that they will be ridiculed.

Surprise, surprise ...

There are five types of surprise:[9]

- Bolt from the blue – a completely unexpected event.
- Expected direction of event is wrong.
- Expected timing of event is wrong.
- Expected duration of event is wrong.
- Expected amplitude of event is wrong.

The bolt from the blue is when the wheels suddenly come off. Such as when an employer suddenly cancels a training contract, a supplier suddenly goes out of business, a firm issues an unexpected profits warning, or some other untoward event occurs. Directional surprises are events that are anticipated, but that emerge from an unexpected quarter. For example, analysts may be expecting a takeover bid, but they are surprised by the bidder's identity. Timing surprises happen when things take longer than expected, or happen faster than expected. For example, Tullow Oil's Jubilee field off West Africa is taking longer than expected to reach full capacity because of production problems. Analysts expected Apple's third-generation iPad to sell in large quantities – but not as many as 3m in the first four days. (The first-generation iPad took 80 days to sell 3m.) Durational surprises happen when decision-makers know what, when and in what order things will occur, but the events last longer or shorter than analysts expected. The "bubble" market in Chinese property has lasted longer than expected. An amplitude surprise is where an event is expected, but proves more or less severe than forecast. For instance, Cove, a UK-listed gas and oil company, expected to find gas in Mozambique. The surprise was the sheer scale of the discovery – almost double the expected find. The common thread linking all five forms of surprise is that they spring from an expectation that proves wrong.

Pleasant surprises may take care of themselves. At the very least they are nice problems to have. Scenario planning can reduce the risk of being caught off-guard by the less pleasant variety. Scenario planning involves posing "what if?" questions. What if the employer breaks the contract? What if the oil proves reluctant to leave the ground? What if a surprise bidder suddenly appears? Scenario planning means that if circumstances change, decision-makers are not just buffered by events but stand a better chance of selecting the optimal path.

Avoiding judgmental traps

The first and possibly most important step in avoiding judgmental traps is to be aware of them. Seeing something one way means not seeing it another way. The second step is to seek out additional information. What are you not seeing? What irrelevant anchors might be informing your estimates? What readily available information may be weighing disproportionately in the balance? Be particularly wary when everything seems to point in one direction. What potentially discomfiting information may have been overlooked? Separate fact from assumption:

- What do I know?

- What do I think I know?
- How do I know?

Past and present are rarely identical – hence the saying that no man ever steps in the same river twice.[10] If two situations seem similar, look for differences between them. Bear in mind that important differences may not be obvious. A snag with the brewery project referred to earlier was that profit margins in large-scale production were much thinner than in small-scale production.

Another technique for teasing out potentially subtle but important differences is to reverse the sense of proportion and see small things as large. For example, RIM's BlackBerry phone reversed the industry standard for delivering e-mail to phones from "pull" to "push". Early on, competitors might have been tempted to regard this innovation as destined to become a technological orphan. The competitive threat becomes more obvious by magnifying the difference between push and pull and then considering the implications – particularly for business users.

All that glitters: evaluating opportunity

All that glitters may not be gold. Yet what appears to be a glittering opportunity is hard to resist. In the Western world, from school days onwards, people are urged to make the most of their opportunities. *Carpe diem* (seize the day), as the saying goes. You may never have the chance again. Yet in business, an opportunity is worth pursuing only if you can make a return on it, otherwise, as the directors of the brewery discovered, and Barclays might have found if it had bought the whole of Lehman Brothers, it becomes a liability. So how do you spot a good opportunity?

First you must have a clear strategy. Although there are many fat textbooks on the subject, strategy simply means deciding how to invest scarce resources. Sound business strategy is just as much about what you don't do as what you do. Don't buy something just because it is cheap.

Don't be too ambitious. The brewery might have sustained a more modest expansion. By going for the big plant, the management overreached themselves. A good way of determining if an opportunity is manageable is to consider how a decision will play out in practice. If this venture goes ahead, what will definitely happen? For instance, if the answer is eight times as much beer to sell, where are the customers? Don't rush important decisions. Stop and think about what the decision means. How will it change things? ING's successful acquisition of Barings offers an important lesson here. Like Lehman, Barings collapsed over a weekend, when it failed to find a buyer. Yet ING refused to be rushed. It did not delay but it took its time, and thoroughly poked and prodded the possibilities before making a commitment – it made haste slowly, in other words.

Time changes everything. It can bring forth possibilities that are obscured by the fog of war. Barclays eventually acquired the best of Lehman for Barclays Capital, its investment-banking arm. The move enabled Barclays Capital to achieve 4–5 years' growth at a stroke. As St Augustine said, "Patience obtaineth all things."

Perfect solutions rarely exist. Usually it is necessary to consider trade-offs. For example, when making procurement decisions, lower engine power may be traded off against increased service life. Speed may be traded for comfort, or vice versa. Some functionality may be sacrificed to keep costs down. It is equally important to know what corners cannot be cut. A rule of thumb here is whether the boundary conditions are met. Half a loaf of bread is better than nothing because it goes some way to relieving appetite. Conversely, half a car is useless. Similarly, if fast travel links are essential but the premises for a new factory are 40 miles from the nearest rail link, then boundary conditions are not met. So the premises should be rejected, no matter how frustrating the search is becoming. No amount of wishful thinking is going to change that inconvenient fact.

Separating heart and head

All decisions are influenced by emotion. Edward de Bono, who came up with and developed the concept of lateral thinking, offers a simple but powerful analytical technique for analysing an opportunity that allows decision-makers to address both heart and head.

It is based on colour-coding their analysis as follows:

■ Blue – thinking about thinking.

- Red – raw emotional reaction to an idea, no justification required.
- Yellow – perceived advantages with reasons.
- Black – risks, doubts, possible snags.
- White – information needed to evaluate an idea.
- Green – where could this idea lead?

The process should start with blue. Thinking about thinking means getting into the right frame of mind. Decision-makers need to decide what they want to achieve. For example, the purpose of the exercise might be to decide whether to make an acquisition or to try to find alternatives to making staff redundant.

Red enables decision-makers to articulate feelings like fear, excitement and vague intuitions without having to rationalise their reactions. It recognises emotion for what it is: for example, that a prima facie opportunity to achieve rapid expansion is exciting.

Yellow involves listing the advantages of an idea and best possible outcomes – but giving reasons. Reasons are required because an opportunity that is superficially attractive may prove to offer few real benefits when subject to more rigorous scrutiny.

Black involves looking for trouble, listing all the disadvantages of an idea and possible snags – such as unknown toxic assets or thinner profit margins. Most decisions fail because of insufficient black strand thinking. An opportunity may have many downsides yet still be worth pursuing. The important thing is that downsides are identified and addressed before a firm commitment is made.

White centres upon information search and making sure that decisions are properly informed. It requires decision-makers to identify what information is needed before making a decision. For instance, Monsanto might have been better prepared for what lay ahead if it had done more homework about the biotechnology industry.

Green is generative. It involves looking at the wider possibilities, and considering what has been learned from the exercise and how that learning can inform strategy. When a firm enters a competitive market sector – such as tablet computers or smartphones – and sales are disappointing, should it continue investing in that market or are there better opportunities to be had?

When not to make a decision

Not all emotional influences are destructive. Although sadness focuses attention upon the self, sad people are generally reflective and therefore less likely to rush into things. Sad people are also more receptive to, and more likely to seek, change. As a rule, however, it is unwise to make an important decision when emotions are running high. Imagine a jar of earth and water. If the jar is shaken, the water becomes cloudy. Given time, the earth settles down and the water is again clear. Similarly, strong emotions cloud judgment so they are best left to subside. Few decisions need to be made immediately. Anger is responsible for many bad decisions. Despondency and exuberance should be seen as opposite sides of the same coin – that is, both wrong.

"Only the paranoid survive"

"It was the last thing we expected," said Peter Baring after the bank collapsed. Surprise reflects the gap between expectations and reality. Although the proverb states that "seeing is believing", errors of judgment are made because believing is seeing.

The best way to avoid confirmation and expectation traps is to search diligently for information that contradicts beliefs. The Bank of England should have been more curious about the rumours surrounding BCCI and other "dead fish". Barings should have checked that Leeson's positions were matched. In the search for contradictory data, decision-makers must be willing to consider that they may be wrong. That may be the hardest bit of all.

Only the Paranoid Survive is Andy Grove's account of how Intel navigated amid changes in the computer industry (Grove was chief executive and chairman of the company). According to the *Oxford Concise Dictionary*, paranoia includes an abnormal tendency to suspect and mistrust. In other words, paranoia is the opposite of overconfidence. Behaving as if paranoid means reacting strongly to small things. It means confronting problems while they are still small and containable. Just as one falling leaf presages autumn, a small, single, untoward event can be highly significant. For instance, if a spanner goes missing on an aircraft carrier, all activity stops until it is found. This is because that spanner, though small in itself, is a symptom of possible disorder. The loss, small as it may seem, contradicts the notion that the ship is safe. The danger is that the "single leaf" is explained away. For instance, in May 2007 UBS suddenly announced a $124m loss following the closure of Dillon Reed Capital Management, a hedge fund spun off from UBS just 18 months earlier. UBS's share price dropped, but only slightly, and recovered within a month. It was as if investors rationalised the "leaf" away, treating it as a unique event, a tiny black mark in the bank's otherwise stellar history. As we now know, the Dillon Reed dead leaf was a symptom of much deeper-rooted problems.

Similarly, one sticky pedal was one too many. If Toyota had "overreacted" at the first signs of trouble by mounting a full-scale investigation, it could have spared itself much anxiety and commercial damage. If the directors of the brewery had dwelt more on the implications of a non-executive director being prepared to resign over an issue, they too might have survived. Acting upon small things also means that decision-makers have more options for dealing with problems. The longer they wait, the more those options narrow.

Finally, the "single leaf" principle can work in reverse. It implies that good decisions can be made with very little information. That is, it is the significance of the information that matters rather than the quantity. One of Sony Classical's most successful artists is Glen Gould, who died in 1982. David Oppenheim, the director of Columbia Masterworks (now Sony Classical), signed Gould to an exclusive contract having heard only one performance. Selecting the *Goldberg Variations* as Gould's debut performance at a time when Bach was respected rather than popular was equally risky. Yet the recording was an immediate success and has never been out of print. Marks & Spencer, a UK retailer, started from a stall in Leeds market. The modern chain might never have existed but for Thomas Spencer's decision to invest his life savings in a partnership with Michael Marks. For Spencer it was a huge risk. All he had to go on was Marks's limited business track record and his energy and dedication. As we now know, it was one of the most successful bets in business history. Moral: bet on the person, not the project.

3 Ghosts and shadows: where is reality?

"We are never deceived, we deceive ourselves."

Goethe

IN APRIL 2010, an oilrig off the Gulf of Mexico operated by BP exploded, killing 11 people. An environmental disaster followed as millions of barrels of oil spilled into the sea. It took three months for the flow of oil to be stemmed. When Tony Hayward, BP's chief executive, heard the news he reportedly said, "How the hell could that happen?"

How indeed? Deepwater drilling was supposed to be safe. Besides, BP had plenty of opportunities to improve the safety of its operations. In 2005, an explosion at its Texas refinery killed 15 people and injured 170. The same year it suffered a major oil spill in Alaska resulting in a forced shutdown of the Prudhoe Bay plant followed by the replacement of 22 miles of corroded pipes. Had BP's management learned nothing from these disasters?[1]

Chapters 1 and 2 focused on how decisions can go awry when individuals have a poor grasp of reality. Yet organisations are prone to the same problems of overconfidence as individuals. Moreover, just as individuals filter information to make sense of their environments, so do organisations. This chapter explores how organisations construct their realities. In theory, firms are forever scanning their environments looking for threats and opportunities. In practice, they generally concoct their environments. Decisions go awry because they take their concoctions seriously and so end up living in a fantasy world. The solution to this problem lies in being less aggressive towards reality by treating it as "useful fiction".

What is a problem?

According to the textbooks, decision-making begins with a problem. The decision-makers' task is to identify all possible solutions and then choose the one that best matches their goal. This model assumes that problems are self-evident, but in the real world problems seldom arrive clearly and accurately labelled. BP had a problem dating back over a decade but failed to recognise it until the rig exploded. Newspapers face an uncertain future. What exactly is the problem? Is it the proliferation of free newspapers, or do free newspapers appeal mainly to people who would otherwise not read a newspaper? Is it the growth of online news? Is it falling advertising revenues? Or is it something else? And how does or might the problem differ between different publications? Similarly, what do sporadic outbreaks of industrial unrest in China mean? Are these just noisy events that occasionally happen to make the headlines or are they weak signals heralding the end of cheap labour? Unless decision-makers diagnose the problem accurately, they may set off in the wrong direction.

What do hierarchies really do?

The textbooks also assume that once problems are recognised, action is taken to address them. The Prudhoe Bay pipeline must have been rusting for a long time before BP ordered an emergency shutdown, as that level of corrosion does not happen overnight. The trouble is that problems are crafty. If they do not cause too much trouble, they will probably be allowed to fester as decision-makers are perpetually distracted by more pressing issues. Indeed, a study by Henry Mintzberg, a professor at the Desautels Faculty of Management at McGill University in Montreal, and colleagues into how decisions are really made in firms found that some problems had been in existence for over a quarter of a century. Citigroup discovered this to its cost. It sold repackaged subprime debt with so-called "liquidity puts" entitling buyers to recoup their money if the market failed. The move was seen as a clever twist to raise charges. It came undone when $25 billion worth of debt suddenly reappeared on the balance sheet. Senior managers allegedly knew nothing of the higher risk being run. The problem may not have remained hidden for 25 years, but it was concealed long enough for the damage to be well and truly done.

Problems are also good at hiding within layers of hierarchy. Organisations can accomplish things that no individual can. They attain their goals via division of labour, enabling complex tasks to be broken down into small, manageable pieces. Hierarchy enables a system of delegation and helps to promote efficiency and control. Yet by definition, hierarchies distance decision-makers from other people's realities. For example, Toyota was reluctant to acknowledge the sticky-pedal problem (see Chapter 1). In 2006, four years before it became a public scandal, junior engineers warned senior management about potentially serious problems. These included the alleged practice of putting pressure on suppliers to cut component prices, the overuse of short-term contractors and an overreliance on computerised safety testing. The warning was apparently ignored because senior management were more interested in pursuing their ambition to overtake Ford as the world's biggest carmaker. Engineers were the first to recognise emerging systemic problems because they were closest to their source.

Solving the wrong problem

Even if the existence of a problem is officially recognised, the definition may be a poor fit with reality. A problem is usually thought of as a difficulty – something to be rid of. BP wanted to get rid of the oil spill. Somali pirates are a problem because they threaten international merchant shipping. Insurers would rather that piracy did not exist. The collapse of supply chains following the 2011 earthquake and tsunami in Japan created huge problems for manufacturers. They wished the problem would disappear and everything would revert to normal. Yet a problem is like a capsule. It contains all sorts of ingredients – fact, fiction, ideology, prejudice, opinion, rumour, overstatement and understatement – all blended together.

This is why problem definition is never an exact science. Much may depend on who defines the problem. For instance, when the first cases of AIDS began to appear in the United States in the early 1980s, different agencies saw different problems. The medical profession saw a new disease affecting gay men. Other health professionals saw AIDS as a lifestyle problem. Religious groups saw it as a punishment for sin. It was a long time before anyone saw the problem for what it was, that is, a global threat to human health. Similarly, cyber-security means different things to different people. Firms worry about threats to servers. Consumers worry about criminals stealing bank and credit card details. The military worry about satellites being attacked. Cyber-security is all these things, and more. It is a multidimensional problem – and one that is far from fully understood. What we see and how we see depends on where we stand. We may think we know the whole of something but our knowledge may turn out to be an illusion.

As noted in Chapter 2, individuals filter information to make sense of their environments. Firms do the same. They filter problems through corporate mindsets. For example, McDonald's and Burger King, and Coca-Cola and Pepsi have tended to see each other as their main rival. It is only fairly recently that they have started to recognise the equally if not more potent threat posed by healthy diet campaigns. A way of seeing is also a way of not seeing.

The invented reality

Since reality is malleable, firms can define problems in a manner that suits their purpose. In 2006 a child in the UK allegedly woke up screaming after eating contaminated chocolate made by Cadbury, a global confectionery company. The contamination was caused by water dripping from a burst pipe. Cadbury allegedly knew about the contamination but company statistics indicated that the risk of anyone contracting salmonella was minuscule. In fact there were over 40 cases. Besides, European law forbids any contamination of a ready-to-eat product. What made Cadbury decide to market the chocolate?

What happens is that the inconvenient elements of a problem are gradually edited out – for instance, the more threatening aspects of a problem are watered down or airbrushed. Consequently the threat disappears. The contaminated chocolate is thus deemed to be fit for human consumption. But this is not because someone has thoroughly investigated the problem and discovered that it is a false alarm. It is because potentially disturbing information gets smoothed out as the problem becomes shaped and officially defined.

Rushing a solution

Even if decision-makers accept that there is a problem, the solution may be a poor match. In a famous paper about how decisions are made in practice, Michael Cohen and colleagues likened organisations to garbage bins.[2] Faced with a problem, the first response is usually to rake in the "bin" and see if there is something that might do. This can be sensible. For instance, instead of going to the trouble and expense of inventing a completely new sports coupé, VW fished in the bin and successfully revived the Sirocco. Similarly, when the British government started formulating plans to sell parts of Royal Bank of Scotland and Lloyds, rather than inventing something completely new, it looked to the defunct Williams & Glyn's Bank (an RBS subsidiary until 1985 when it was merged with its parent) and Trustee Savings Bank (owned by Lloyds) brands under which those parts could be sold. When Kleinwort Benson replotted its strategy following the global financial crisis, it decided to return to its 200-year-old roots and revived the old-fashioned merchant-banking model, providing independent advice to individuals, companies and governments.

The trouble is that few ready-made solutions exactly match requirements. When searching for something that will do, decision-makers may try to apply solutions that prove to be a poor fit with the problem. BP made this mistake when it tried to use a large containment dome, known as a cofferdam, to collect the leaking oil from the Gulf of Mexico oilrig. The argument in favour of the cap was that it was an "off-the-shelf" component, ready for immediate use, whereas other solutions would take time. Although BP apparently rated the chance of success as between "medium" and "high", outside experts disagreed. In the event the off-the-shelf solution failed. BP should have opted for a custom-built solution from the start. But it was by no means unique in trying the ready-made solution. Research by Henry Mintzberg and colleagues has shown that firms seldom opt for custom-built solutions until all else has failed. However, they could often save time in the long run by starting with a clean sheet.[3]

Solving problems that do not exist

Firms can also waste time and energy solving problems that do not exist. Between 2003 and 2004, Lego's sales fell by almost 50%. As part of its plan to try to revive its fortunes, the toy company reviewed its operations and interviewed customers about their requirements. Lego discovered that it had been focusing on the wrong problem. It had expended huge resources making daily deliveries to customers who did not want them. Lego's mistake was confusing frequency with reliability. That is, it assumed that efficient meant delivering every day. Yet what customers really valued was dependability.

Similarly, Boeing and Airbus seem to regard one another as "the problem", that is, their main competitive threat. So they direct their energies to trying to outdo one another in building large planes. Neither seems overly concerned by the activities of firms like Bombardier and Irkus, which specialise in manufacturing single-aisle planes. Yet these smaller aircraft account for a large proportion of the total aviation market and are the preferred choice of low-cost carriers. Firms like individuals are prone to myopia.

Subtle movements

The textbooks say that one of the major challenges of business strategy is coping with an inherently turbulent environment. Similarly, one of the clichés of modern business is that the only constant is change. Together these perspectives paint a tumultuous picture of business life. The environment, we learn, is in a constant state of upheaval and firms are forever straining to adapt. Yet important shifts do not always advertise themselves. The hotel industry has certainly experienced turbulence in the wake of the global financial crisis. But a more profound development has been the emergence of online booking agencies like Late Rooms, which have undermined the traditional business model of fixed tariffs. They have also made customers more powerful by enabling them to compare prices and facilities, read reviews and write them with ease. Similarly, online betting enables bets to be placed on things like the next penalty or corner while a game is being played. The result has been to change the dynamics of the gambling industry. The point is that the most important changes in the operating environment may not make headline news. They are often seen in the subtle movements and oblique shifts that are barely perceptible at first and therefore easily overlooked.

Corporate myopia

Yet even when environmental clues become more obvious, firms may be slow to react. Myopia develops because the filters used to scan the environment reflect what a firm sees as important. Kodak saw itself as mainly in the business of film cameras and accessories. Digital photography was none of its business. Similarly, at first Microsoft saw search engines like Google and Yahoo! as irrelevant. By the time Kodak and Microsoft recognised the threat, competitors had stolen a decisive lead.

The same goes for recruitment policies, training plans, remuneration systems, marketing, pricing and public-relations activities and so on. They are all geared to support what a firm sees as its core business. As digital photography gained momentum, Kodak continued to recruit research and development scientists interested in conventional cameras. Similarly, despite the trend towards more economical cars, Subaru has not rushed to adapt. It bases its appeal on iconic boxer engines and advertisements showing its thirsty cars pulling big trucks out of snowdrifts. Subaru is likely to continue to recruit engineers interested in producing rally cars, thus maintaining the status quo when the time may be ripe for change. The hugely successful Apple iPad was foreshadowed by the iPod Touch, which appeared several years before the iPad was launched – a huge span of opportunity for competitors to enter the market for tablet computing. The opportunity was lost because firms such as Acer, HP, Dell and Samsung were riveted to conventional keyboard computers powered by Windows operating systems. Their defences were like imaginary Maginot lines, formidable but trained in the wrong direction.

Reality as myth

In summary, what firms call reality is more accurately described as myth. A myth is a theory of the world. It represents the received view of reality; the official formulation of "what is" and what should be done. For instance, synthetic chemicals are often regarded as "bad" whereas natural substances are seen as "good". This is a myth because the world is full of toxic and carcinogenic compounds that occur naturally. Out-of-town shopping was seen as a solution to city-centre congestion. But rising fuel prices are putting pressure on that myth. Similarly, the banking sector promulgates the myth that big bonuses are essential to retain suitably qualified and experienced investment bankers. A firm's definition of its core competence is likewise a myth. All myths are partly true. Therefore all myths are partly false.

It is the part that is false that should concern us. The Land Rover is popularly regarded as farmers' vehicle of choice. Indeed, some farmers drive Land Rovers. But some farmers drive vehicles made by other manufacturers such as Mitsubishi. Deepwater drilling is deemed to be safe. Yet what do we mean by safe? There had been fatal accidents in the offshore oil business before Deepwater Horizon. Yet we want to believe in the myth that deepwater drilling is safe because we need the oil. The rationale for outsourcing call centres to India and other low-cost countries is that it is cheaper and the quality of customer service is unimpaired. The first part of the myth may be true, but what about the second part?

Some car manufacturers pour resources into flagship models, such as Audi's RS6 with its 580-horsepower V10 Lamborghini engine and Nissan's twin turbo V6 GT-R. Sales are minuscule. The myth is that these so-called "halo cars" help promote the rest of the brand. Perhaps they do, but they also suck in resources that could perhaps be put to better use. Besides, other firms like Honda and VW seem to manage without them.

The ruling myth

Firms can be seen as riddled with myths competing for dominance. A ruling myth reflects the official viewpoint about what constitutes reality, what is, or is not a problem, and what should be done. BP was shocked by the Deepwater Horizon disaster because it thought it had learned from earlier accidents. Management believed that they had instilled a safety culture in the organisation. Like all myths, that was the official belief. Moreover, the assumption was partly true. BP had invested a lot in personal safety. The disaster happened because BP paid insufficient attention to process safety including effective liaison with subcontractors like Halliwell and Transocean.

Although techniques have improved since the days of earlier accidents, deepwater drilling remains hazardous. To paraphrase the official report, the intricate judgments, calculations and trade-offs required to maintain safety mean that even under optimal conditions, things can go wrong. All the hard hats provided and precautions taken were necessary but insufficient to guarantee safety. Yet the myth that gained credence in BP was that a safety culture existed – but there may have been people in the firm who believed that the risk was bigger than what was officially recognised and who represented a competing myth.

Mythical rights and wrongs

Myths are useful because they stop firms from overreacting to minor disturbances. For example, a chief executive scrutinising a set of accident statistics may say: "We are sorry that someone has cut their thumb on a stapling machine, but it isn't going to make us change our business plan." Indeed not. The trouble is that ruling myths can be immensely resilient in the face of contradictory information. For instance, as sales of carbonated drinks tumbled, Pepsi embraced the myth that it needed to reinvent itself by selling healthier products such as porridge oats, sports drinks and fruit juices. These products may account for 20% of Pepsi's total sales. But analysts question the disproportionate amount of effort Pepsi made to promote them. They say it have may have hurt the rest of the business. Yet Pepsi plans to triple the revenues from its healthier products by 2020. Clearly, the myth still commands credence. That does not mean it is right or wrong – only that it is resilient.

To be more precise, a ruling myth holds sway as long as it can account for a sufficient portion of reality. In his book *The Structure of Scientific Revolutions,* Thomas Kuhn shows how hard it can be for new and better theories to become accepted.[4] Scientists who have built careers developing existing theory may fiercely resist new ideas and it takes a huge amount of evidence to discredit outmoded paradigms. The same goes for ruling myths. The UK National Health Service's £12 billion IT project to provide every patient in England with a personal electronic record was an ambitious and controversial idea and a huge technical challenge, involving legal and ethical issues. It was not long before the project was hit by delays and cost overruns. In 2006 the myth that all was well was contradicted when Accenture, one of the project's four big suppliers, withdrew at huge cost to the company. Two years later, the myth was challenged again when another supplier, Fujitsu, was sacked. Yet it was not until 2010 that the project was suspended. By then it was already over four years late and has since been cancelled.

New strategies (competing myths) are like new scientific theories. They must challenge and disprove the value of existing strategies if they are to take over and provide a new basis for action. This may not be easy because established strategies are tried, tested and protected by batteries of supporting data. A huge amount of contradictory evidence may be needed to mount a successful challenge. An example is this pronouncement by Coca-Cola: "Consumers, including Diet Coke drinkers, are increasingly looking for more beverage options." As Tim Harford, an economist, says, it is the sort of statement that people start to believe if they have worked for Coca-Cola for too long. Yet such rhetoric can exert a powerful hold over firms because it becomes the "taken-for-granted" basis for action. Incidentally, competing myths are also partial truths. For instance, encouraging individual health authorities to develop their own electronic patient record systems means that different systems will be unable to interact with one another. This is the very problem that the national system was designed to overcome. Eventually this new myth may crumble as inefficiencies manifest themselves.

Sometimes it takes a severe shock to discredit a myth. The explosion at Chernobyl in 1979 destroyed the myth that nuclear power is safe – although many people say it is if proper processes are followed. But then there are earthquakes and tsunamis, as in Japan in 2011.

Collapsing share prices destroyed the myth that all was well with Enron and Lehman Brothers. The explosion at Deepwater Horizon destroyed the myth that BP had instilled a strong safety culture. In other words, a crisis means that a ruling myth is no longer credible because it cannot account for a sufficient portion of reality.

Go slow to go fast

Problem definition matters because so many things flow from it. It may therefore be wise to devote more time to studying the problem. In his book *Zen in the Art of Archery*, Eugen Herrigel tells us that we should avoid aiming at the target for a long time and focus on developing more fundamental knowledge about what we are trying to achieve, and the means of achieving it.[5] Then, when we eventually fire the arrow, we are much more likely to hit the target.

It is a lesson that may stand Chevron, a multinational energy corporation, in good stead. As supplies of "easy oil" dry up, Saudi Arabia and Kuwait have turned to the billions of barrels of heavy oil lying beneath the desert. Heavy oil can be as thick as black treacle. It is therefore more difficult and more expensive to extract and refine than light oil. Not everyone believes that the experiment led by Chevron to extract the 25 billion barrels trapped in the Wafra field between Kuwait and Saudi Arabia will succeed. Chevron is certainly taking a risk as it is funding the estimated $10 billion project. Yet it seems to be approaching the project sensibly, treating it like a chemistry experiment, studying the problem and the technology needed to solve it before deciding whether to go beyond the pilot stage. Bill Higgs, Chevron's head of operations in Saudi Arabia, says: "You know where the oil is ... There's no doubt about that. So the question is: how do I economically produce it?" Chevron may not know the answer yet, but at least it is asking the right question.

The problem behind the problem

Look for the problem behind the problem. Arresting a few Somali pirates will treat only the symptoms, not the disease. The disease is rooted in those who alert pirates to valuable cargo passing through coastal waters off Somalia. Ships carrying grain are seldom hijacked.

Pirates prefer to target ships carrying flat-screen televisions and other expensive items. Behind the pirates lies a criminal, but professional, network that issues ransom demands, receives payment and launders the proceeds of crime. Providing ships with an armed escort may mean fewer attacks, but it does not address the underlying problem. Now piracy has become a form of organised crime – an illegal industry but a sophisticated one.

Companies like Lockheed and BAE Systems, both in the defence business, have a problem. Defence budgets are being cut. The obvious solution is to reduce dependence on government contracts by selling to other markets. Yet when this option was tried in similar circumstances in the 1980s, it failed. It failed because defence firms benefit from governments' notoriously inefficient procurement processes. If these firms had paused for long enough to develop a more fundamental knowledge of the problem, instead of grasping the seemingly obvious solution, they might have realised that working for firms more exposed to market disciplines than public-sector organisations was bound to be less profitable and that they needed to address underlying problems of efficiency first. As the global financial crisis subsided, banks tried to entice investors back into the market by offering them incentives. Virgin Money was more successful because it recognised that the real problem was rebuilding consumer confidence. By studying the problem behind the problem, Virgin Money saw that incentives could drive customers away by stirring fears of history repeating itself.

Listening to Galileo: conceptual blockbusting

Often it is the way we think about problems that stops us from seeing a solution. Soap powder is useful, yet what we really want is not something that washes whiter, as such, but clean clothes. If we assume that planes need pilots, we will never invent unmanned aircraft. If we always associate guns with bullets, we will never imagine lasers and an end to armies having to transport munitions. While we think of computers necessarily being linked by wires, we will never imagine bluetooth technology. While we associate air bags with cars, we may never think of fitting them to motorbikes as Honda was the first to do.

An interesting experiment is to displace the central idea – the one big assumption that dictates thinking. By questioning the popular assumption that Earth was at the centre of the universe, Galileo realised that Earth was round and circled the sun. On a less profound note, burger outlets wrestled with falling sales until they realised that "fast" food need not mean unhealthy food. By displacing that central idea, they were able to envisage offering salads and other healthier choices. Hybrid vehicles displace the central assumption that cars run on petrol. If BP had recognised that its approach to safety was too centred on the physical safety of people, the Deepwater Horizon accident might have been avoided. Similarly, a frequent error in negotiated decisions is assuming that one party's gains must represent another's losses. In other words, if an outcome is good for one party, it must, by definition, be bad for the other party – a zero-sum game. Such restricted thinking means that negotiators focus on how to divide the metaphorical pie instead of thinking of ways to expand it by inventing options that are good for both parties. Sometimes it is not the problem that defeats us but the assumptions we make about how to solve it.

Second-order thinking

Applying second-order thinking can solve seemingly intractable problems. First-order thinking involves trying to solve a problem within existing parameters. In contrast, second-order thinking involves stepping outside existing parameters. When computers were the size of rooms, people tried to make the hardware smaller. The result of applying such first-order thinking was that computers became a bit smaller. The real breakthrough was recognising that if the software required less space, the hardware would shrink automatically – second-order thinking. Similarly, it once took weeks to load and unload cargo ships. Small efficiencies were achieved by better stowing and handling of goods – first-order thinking. Containers (second-order thinking) were a mini industrial revolution because they involved a lot less paperwork and reduced loading and unloading times to a few hours, cutting costs to a fraction of their former levels.

Robots are useful. They act as first responders in emergencies by entering areas that are too dangerous to send people into. They can defuse bombs. They are even being developed to help elderly people move around their homes. Robots can also make businesses more efficient. They are cheaper than humans and work better. For instance, ScanCom, a Danish firm that makes wooden garden furniture, uses robots at its plant in Vietnam for drilling and sanding operations. A few robots and one supervisor can do the work of 50 people. Amazon uses robots for transporting packages from shelves to operatives. First-order solutions for improving efficiency are either to build robots that can perform many more operations, or to modify operations so that robots can perform them. A second-order solution is to make the robots redundant by eliminating the work they perform: for example, using wood that does not need to be sanded, and re-engineering operations so goods no longer have to be transported.

Stop problems before they start

Clever organisations anticipate potential problems and take preventative action. Faber-Castell pre-empted expensive lawsuits by refashioning its pencils using non-toxic materials to stop children from being poisoned. Aspartame, a synthetic sweetener, which has been linked to serious health problems, is used by many food and beverage companies – but not by, for example, Sainsbury's. Pipe joins are weak spots precisely because they can leak. Forethought and a minor piece of re-engineering could have saved Cadbury from the contamination problem it suffered when water leaked onto a chocolate production line. When the Rolls-Royce engine on flight QF32 exploded shortly after taking off from Singapore, Australian carrier Qantas immediately grounded its entire fleet of six A380s super-jumbos as a precaution. It was a wise move because parts of the engine disintegrated and pierced the casing. Such uncontained engine failure could have caused much bigger problems if components had penetrated the passenger cabin. It seems obvious, yet other airlines kept their A380s flying pending checks. Solving nascent problems is better than waiting for them to emerge full-blown.

Similarly, if manufacturers had to pay to dispose of their products and for the damage they cause to human health, they might make them in different ways. For example, they might need to find better ways to make disposable nappies, or stop using plastic bottles for water and other drinks, or take the salt out of crisps. Unilever makes detergents that use little water and rinse off easily – an important innovation as water becomes scarcer. Alcoa is attempting to measure its environmental impacts, which may help it to deal with any subsequent legislation and to capitalise on government subsidies that might become available.

Solve the right problem

On a happier note, business history has shown that fortunes can be made by directing resources to the right problem. Henry Ford made motor cars affordable. Swatch did the same for watches. IKEA successfully addressed the problem of supplying cheap, attractive furnishing. Having fallen far behind industry leaders in the smartphone market, Samsung concentrated on making middle-range handsets for people unable to afford high-end smartphones. Lesson: pursuit of the unattainable is at the expense of the possible.

Apply the "because" test

"How do you know?" questions help to inject rigour into debate. Another useful discipline is to make sure the answer contains the word "because". It forces decision-makers to justify their assertions. It is a form of evidence-based decision-making that can expose woolly thinking and vague, untested assumptions. Evidence-based does not mean evidence-biased. A decision is evidence-based when the following four conditions are met:

- Claims are supported with data.
- The limits of the data are understood.
- The approach to interpretation is clear.
- Contradictory data are also considered.

A decision is evidence-biased when decision-makers use their information selectively.

A word of caution: we make assumptions without realising it. For instance, the taxi rank at London's Paddington station was repositioned to make way for the new Crossrail station. The traditional black cabs coped with the change. The first Mercedes Vito cab to use the new ramp had a less than happy experience. It is only a few centimetres wider than the black cab, but too wide to negotiate the ramp comfortably. The problem reflects an unchecked assumption. All cats may be grey in the dark, but not all cabs are the same. Incidentally, the new ramp caused chaos when it was first opened. Taxis could not clear the traffic lights quickly enough because the lights had not been resequenced. Consequently, enormous traffic jams developed with passengers running up substantial charges on the meter before they had even left the station. As a taxi driver said, it probably all looked marvellous when modelled on the computer.

Finding the lobster: the importance of mind states

Irish folklore holds that lobsters are often found where they are least expected. The same applies to problem solving. Psychologists distinguish between "telic" and "paratelic" frames of mind. In a telic state of mind, we are highly focused upon the task at hand. This means we see it as a means to an end, rather than an end in itself. For example, we may read a report not for pleasure or out of interest, but to appear informed for a meeting. In contrast, in a paratelic mind state, activity is an end in itself. We do things not for any particular purpose but for enjoyment. Although we can move from one mind state to another, we cannot be telic and paratelic simultaneously.

Logically, we might expect a telic mind state, with its emphasis on "think, think, think", to be more conducive to problem solving than a paratelic mind state. Yet psychologists believe that the opposite is true. In an experiment with a board game involving 300,000 possible ways of combining pieces, but only one correct way, paratelics did better than telics, even though they were just playing with the pieces, arranging them into shapes rather than trying to find the solution to the problem. This may explain why many decision-makers claim to get their best ideas on the golf course or in the bath.

Expecting the unexpected

One thing to reflect on in the bath is where the next crisis is likely to come from, when the gap between myth and reality will no longer be sustainable. By then it is often too late and the damage is done.

Yet there are usually plenty of warnings that the ruling myth is no longer credible. A surprise is anything that we did not expect. In their book *Managing the Unexpected*, Karl Weick and Kathleen Sutcliffe say:[6]

> To have an expectation is to envision something ... that is reasonably certain to come about. To expect something is to be mentally ready for it.

The best way to avoid unpleasant surprises is to be on the lookout for feedback that contradicts the ruling myth. Particular attention should be paid to small incidents that are inconsistent with expectations. They may just be noise, but they may be signals of an impending crisis. What information might have been dismissed too readily or even ignored altogether? As Weick and Sutcliffe say:

> Expectations act like an invisible hand that guides you towards soothing perceptions that confirm your hunches, and away from troublesome ones that don't. But it's these very same troublesome perceptions that foreshadow surprises.

Computer testing should make engineers' lives easier. Yet Toyota's engineers were anxious to change a regime that, in theory, should suit them. It is an example of a troubling perception, a small disturbance that foreshadowed a much bigger problem.

Fact or fiction?

Guarding against surprise means treating what others call reality as "useful fiction". That is, as inherently false but capable of serving as a tentative platform for action. For instance, the immediate cause of the Deepwater Horizon explosion was a build-up of dangerous gases. BP's senior management knew that the information systems used by engineers stationed on the rig met industry standards. That was correct. Yet what they may not have known was that safety depended upon those working in the control room (who might be nearing the end of a 12-hour shift) noticing minute changes in the stream of data constantly flickering on the computer screen. In other words, there was no automatic warning system. So although senior management may have regarded those systems as safe because they met industry standards, the reality was that they were flawed because the warning signs were missed. In other words, there was a gap between the corporate view of safety (dominant myth) and the daily operational challenges (competing myth) that the systems were unfitted to meet. That gap caused the disaster. The lesson is to guard against placing too much faith in the official view of reality without testing it.

Testing reality

As noted earlier, a myth is a theory of the world. Just as scientists must invent experiments that allow them to test their theories, decision-makers need to devise tests that will enable them to determine a myth's credibility. For example, to test the myth that outsourcing call centres is a good idea, try making ghost calls in person. Do the results inspire confidence? If not, why not? Similarly, some universities define themselves as research led. For that to be true we might expect that at least 51% of income should come from research. If, say, a simple pie chart reveals that 95% of income comes from teaching, the perception of a research-led university is indeed a myth. Likewise, one way of testing the myth that farmers drive Land Rovers is to visit an agricultural auction and see how many Land Rovers there are in the car park compared with agricultural vehicles made by firms such as Mitsubishi and Nissan.

Change the angle of approach by asking frame-breaking questions. Just as the true test of what something is worth is whether the seller is willing to buy it back. Instead of conducting customer surveys, focus research on those who did not buy. Those who pay inflated prices for gold should ask themselves why. Gold may glisten but it has no yield and little utility value except when fashioned into items such as rings and bracelets. So what makes gold valuable?

Imagine a decision being reflected back in a different context. A lawyer, seeing his love-struck sibling writing a long letter to her beloved, says, "Think how that would sound read out in court."

Thinking about how a potentially hostile party might represent an action is a good discipline. Cadbury discovered this to its cost when counsel read out the story about the child who woke up screaming. Similarly, think how feeble the claim that "the system meets industry standards" might sound read out in court, with 11 people dead, unprecedented pollution and billions of dollars' worth of damage. Have loose but well-thought-out contingency plans in place to respond to crises. Firefighters do not know where the next fire will be, but they know that there will be a fire somewhere so they prepare accordingly. Thus when a crisis occurs there is likely to be less pressure to seize upon a poor solution.

"How the hell could that happen?" The best protection against the unexpected is to maintain a sense of uncertainty. Being imbued with doubt is healthy. Doubt need not prevent decision-makers from making risky decisions. It just makes it more likely that they will pause for long enough to consider "unknown unknowns". This is particularly important when things seem to be going well. The calm before the storm may simply mean that the filters are doing their job well, screening out anything that might upset the idyll. There is always something that you do not know. One of the arts of decision-making is knowing that you do not know.

4 Gorilla in the room: information and decision-making

> *"Power, in the business of tomorrow, will flow to those who have the best information about the limits of their information."*
>
> Alvin Toffler

BEFORE THE ADVENT OF ELECTRONIC TRANSMISSION, the fastest way that a written communication could travel was by horseback. Edicts entrusted to papal envoys were never addressed to specific individuals for fear that they might die before the message reached them – a sensible precaution when a message sent from Rome could take two months to reach London. Cargo ships set sail with no precise date for their arrival at their destination and no means of reporting their whereabouts to merchants awaiting delivery. The telegraph was a profoundly important invention because it enabled instantaneous transmission – hence, for example, the railway station's telegraph office and the now defunct telegram. In contrast, we now live in an information-rich world. Yet decision-makers may not be any the wiser as a result.

It has been suggested in earlier chapters that decisions go awry because decision-makers lose sight of reality. In theory, management information systems should counter this problem. Yet in practice they can make things worse. Information systems can lead decision-makers into a hermetically sealed world. Everything seems to be under control, yet this belief may be an illusion. This chapter explains why seemingly rational information systems can mislead and what decision-makers can do to stay in touch with reality. The main lesson is that a way of seeing is also a way of not seeing.

How do we know what we think we know?

It is a fact of organisational life that as information passes up the hierarchy, it becomes more and more refined. Beyond shop-floor level, decision-makers rarely see raw data. Their information will normally have been sieved through many filters so that they can work at a high level of abstraction.

A more subtle problem resides in the nature of knowledge itself. Much of what we know (or think we know) is known by its relationship to something else.[1] For instance, we say "time is money" and "the mind is like a machine" and allude to the computer as having a "virus". These images may not be literally true, but they help us to comprehend our world. For instance, time may not literally be money, but likening time to money helps us understand that the passage of time may not be without cost. The computer does not actually have a virus, but the image enables us to grasp the potentially contagious nature of computer malfunctioning. Crucially, all images are partial representations. For instance, notions of mind as a machine highlight the mind's computational and analytical abilities. But the image says nothing about the mind's creative and intuitive powers. In short, our images reveal, but they also conceal.

The trouble is that we are in danger of forgetting about what is concealed. We forget because some images become so deeply ingrained that we end up taking them literally. When we think of time we usually imagine a "clock". Clocks are everywhere. Clients are charged by the hour. Blue-collar workers are paid an hourly rate. The meeting is scheduled to start at ten o'clock in the morning. It is expected to last for two hours. Another meeting is scheduled for two o'clock. To see time through the prism of the clock is to see it as something that always moves forwards. Part of Stephen Hawking's genius was his realisation that physicists had allowed their thinking about the nature of time to be constrained by the image of the clock. Reconceptualising time as moving backwards as well as forwards enabled Hawking to imagine the cosmos as collapsing backwards in time and things being sucked in to "black holes". In other words, if we are not careful the image becomes *the* way of seeing and thinking about something when it is only *a* way of seeing and thinking.

Similarly, we think of organisations as "machines" or as "systems". For instance, we say a project is "going like clockwork". We describe a process as functioning like a "well-oiled machine". We may lack the "machinery" to pay ad-hoc expenses. We sometimes refer to faltering projects as "black holes". Although these projects are not black holes as physicists understand them, the image encapsulates the notion of projects that suck in huge amounts of resources, yet nothing useful ever emerges (see Chapter 8). When things grind to a halt, we say "the system has crashed". Yet these familiar images can eclipse other ways of seeing. In his book *Images of Organization*, Gareth Morgan shows what these familiar images obscure by invoking new possibilities.[2] For example, mechanistic imagery inhibits our ability to make organisations more agile. In other words, to see something one way is not to see it another way.

Where the unexpected come from

Management information is likewise only a way of seeing. To be more precise, management information often involves substituting part for whole. For example, a firm may be represented by an organisation chart. The chart is useful because it enables outsiders to grasp the scale of the organisation and understand how it is meant to work. Yet it reveals nothing about the informal arrangements – the unofficial alliances, the power vacuums, the cliques, cabals and coalitions – that are every bit as real and as important as what is represented on the chart. A firm's website is a source of information. Yet no matter how good the website may be, it is not the living, breathing firm. The danger is that we forget this. We see the website and think we know the firm. But we know it only through the prism of the website.

In short, the representation is not the reality. The land is always larger than the map so there is always much that is excluded and becomes surplus reality. The danger is that the surplus reality is forgotten and the representation becomes the reality. It is the gap between the representation and the reality that produces the unexpected: the black swans, the nasty white ones and other unlooked for varieties.

Flawed perceptions explain many expensive policy failures. For instance, journalists have described the Kibera suburb of Nairobi as one of the world's worst slums. It is not difficult to see why. There are over 175,000 people crammed into a small shanty town of mud huts and crude corrugated-iron shelters. There is no sewerage and no piped water. Officials in Nairobi talk about bulldozing Kibera. Opponents of the idea argue that wholesale demolition would destroy everything that is good about the community. They say Kibera should not be thought of as a slum with all its connotations of hopelessness, but as a reservoir of pent-up energy, enterprise and creativity. In this view policy should be directed towards self-help, such as investing in better road facilities and sanitation to help release Kibera's potential.

Similarly, designing products and services on the basis of "added value" can result in expensive features that customers seldom use. Designing with the idea of less in mind may be a better way of actually adding value. People are usually happier with things that are less expensive, less difficult to use, less big or heavy, and so on.

Risk as a mirror of imagination

There has been increasing awareness of the need for risk-management systems as a result of a string of high-profile corporate scandals since the 1970s. The argument for their introduction was that firms could eliminate unpleasant surprises by gathering, categorising and capturing information about important risks, assessing their severity and the probability of the risk materialising, determining acceptable levels of risk, and specifying measures for reducing incidence and impact. In other words, a new myth gained credence, that is, that risk is something that can be brought under control.

The main bureaucratic instrument for controlling risk is typically the risk register. Just as our understanding of time may be constrained by the image of the clock, risk registers can become the way of seeing risk, when they are really only one way of seeing. We can study human psychology by observing the behaviour of rats, but we must be aware that the cost of taking this approach is that human psychology becomes reduced to the behaviour of rats. The system of risk registers takes elusive, subtle, dynamic and unpredictable hazards, with all their complex social, economic and psychological connotations, and translates them into a system of notation comprising word-processed descriptors, numerical probabilities, arrows and the like. In other words, the system of notation depicts risk as something that can be known, predicted and managed. Risk may have other ideas. As the following example shows, risk is like water. It seeps through the hairline cracks in an organisation's defences and splits them wide open.

A firm had a business-continuity plan stipulating that if the building had to be evacuated, staff would be sent home and voicemail would be used. If the disruption continued for more than half a day, staff would be moved to a different location. The water supply failed one morning. Within an hour or so, the building became uninhabitable because the washrooms were not working. The water company advised management that supplies would be restored by the following morning. Accordingly, 1,000 staff went home and voicemail was switched on. The next morning the water was still off. Management were assured that it would be on by midday. Again, voicemail was used and staff instructed to return that afternoon. But the water was still off. The water company said it would definitely be on by the following morning. And so it continued. This stop/go state of affairs cost the company three days' business.

We can define risk as the probability of an event multiplied by its impact. For example, as ships become ever larger the probability of an accident may not increase much, but the impact is likely to be more serious because of the difficulties of evacuating thousands of passengers in an emergency. This point was dramatically illustrated in January 2012 when a cruise ship, the *Costa Concordia*, struck a rock and capsized, with the loss of 32 of its 4,200 passengers. Images of the ship were broadcast all over the world. Another ominous but less well-publicised incident occurred just a month or so earlier in a Brazilian port, Punta da Madeira. The *Vale Beijing*, a 361-metre ore carrier (the largest dry-bulk carrier to be built), was being loaded for its maiden voyage when the hull cracked and water gushed in. How could this happen when sophisticated computer modelling had been used to calculate stresses and strains on the new class of ships?

Risk does not always lend itself to neat calculation. The probability of subprime borrowers defaulting was high. Yet individual banks may have given the likely impact of default a low score, because the debt had been chopped up, repackaged and sold on to other banks as collaterised debt obligations. Since almost all subprime lenders were using this strategy, however, these comfortingly low scores concealed a huge systemic risk. We behave as if risk scores are scientifically accurate when they are usually just guesswork.

Perception is reality

It is axiomatic that what seems real is treated as real. Just as a cigarette smoker may not worry about fuel cans labelled "empty" being unaware that the cans are full of explosive vapour, decision-makers are likely to see the representation of risk as real and behave accordingly. Moreover, as decision-makers pore over their registers, diligently ticking off risks, adjusting a probability score here and an impact score there, they may think that they are managing risk. Yet their approach is dictated by the system of notation that prefigures their way of seeing risk in the first place. Cadbury claimed that the contamination detected by its own testing was at 100th of the level deemed dangerous by its scientists. Prosecutors disagreed with this self-serving rationale because European law forbids any contamination of a ready-to-eat product. Moreover, Cadbury focused only on its way of seeing risk, that is, as represented by statistics. It forgot about all the other social, legal and reputational connotations of risk. They were surplus reality – until that reality bit the company.

Gorilla in the room

The same observations apply to many other forms of management information including balanced scorecards. These are systems of notation that purport to provide a more holistic view of an organisation's performance than that given by financial data alone. More precisely, the system of notation comprises a series of metrics, such as how long it takes to answer telephones, process claims, reply to customer complaints and issue contracts. The metrics allow decision-makers to compare actual performance against targets.

Again, the information system relies upon data that will not give the whole picture. The system of scorecards takes performance and reduces it to what can be conveniently and accurately measured. Again, it is not what that recorded information reveals, but what it conceals. For instance, average response times can conceal outliers where callers have been kept waiting for hours; and even though calls may be answered promptly, this does not mean that the person answering the call was helpful and knowledgeable. Yet these metrics make it easy for decision-makers to conclude that the company is providing a good service. Psychologists call it "the gorilla in the room" or situational blindness. That is, managers become so absorbed in their charts, graphs and spreadsheets that they fail to notice looming threats on the horizon.

Not only is there an issue of what counts as data; decision-makers also have to decide what data counts. Inevitably, there is a temptation to dismiss outliers as inconsequential. Yet those extreme but relatively rare incidents may be the outcroppings of deep-seated, latent problems, or early-warning signs of an ageing system beginning to fail. Outliers are data and therefore always worth investigating.

Complicit computers

Computers amplify the danger. This is because software dictates what counts as information and what information counts. Information that cannot be machine processed becomes part of the surplus reality.[3] Yet those other "ways of knowing" such as intuition, rumour, subversive talk, odd thoughts, feelings and flashes of insight may offer a more accurate picture of reality than the graphs, spreadsheets and word-processed reports that comprise the decision-makers official information. For instance, when the trillion-dollar American subprime mortgage market collapsed in 2008/09, in a special report on the future of finance published in January 2009 *The Economist* noted:

> *Mortgage originators, keen to automate their procedures, stopped giving potential borrowers lengthy interviews because they could not easily quantify the firmness of someone's handshake or the fixity of their gaze. Such things turned out to be better predictors of default than credit scores ... but investors at the end of a long chain of securities could not monitor lending decisions.*

Similarly, long before the sticky accelerator-pedal problem occurred (see Chapter 1), Toyota's engineers had expressed concern about overreliance on computers for testing vehicle components. Computer testing has its place. Yet as the engineers recognised, computer testing is not the same as being able to "feel the metal".

Liars in service of truth

Emphatically, more detailed information is not the answer. Elaboration means more of the same and it just makes things worse. For example, more elaborate risk registers and more elaborate scorecards are likely to result in decision-makers spending even more time scrutinising the same narrow channels of information. Besides, excessive information just adds to the illusion of control. Research has shown that the more information we have, the more confident we feel about decisions. Quantity can never substitute for quality.

Quality does not reside in having the most information. Effective decision-making is about being able to sense the limits of information, treating it as a "liar in service of truth". If we are sceptical to begin with, we are more likely to be aware of the gap between the representation and the reality. A different analogy is letter-writing as a means of conveying information. A writes a letter to B describing a foreign country. B then visits the country expecting it to be as A described it. B will probably be either pleasantly surprised or disappointed because the experience will not be like what was described in the letter. You might say the answer is simple. Accept the limitations of what can be conveyed in a letter. This is good advice, but why is the letter likely to be such a poor guide to reality? Common sense says that it is a question of abstraction, that is, what is left out of the model (letter). A deeper problem is that which cannot be conveyed through the medium of language. In this view the letter does not describe reality; it creates it. Although it may be useful for decision-makers to be more aware of the limitations of their information, it is not just a question of what gets left out. Decision-makers need to treat their information as fiction and be aware not so much of what has been left out but what might be subtly different, and of the uncertainties surrounding the information behind the information system. Michael

John Polanyi, a philosopher, makes the point more eloquently:[4]

> *The idea of strictly explicit knowledge is indeed self-contradictory;
> deprived of their tacit coefficients, all spoken words, all formulae, all
> maps and graphs are strictly meaningless. An exact mathematical
> theory means nothing unless we recognise an inexact non-
> mathematical knowledge on which it bears and a person whose
> judgment upholds that bearing.*

Shut the toolbox and open the mind

This still leaves the question of how to deal with the gap between the representation and the reality. The gap can never be closed completely. The best that can be hoped for is to narrow it. One way of doing this is to hold some meetings where risk registers, balanced scorecards and all the other paraphernalia of decision support systems are banned. Instead discuss issues like risk and performance directly. Let "surplus reality" emerge by allowing people to talk in an unstructured fashion instead of following set agendas and processes. Let the imagination and senses get to work – by thinking about possible "unknown unknowns".

Unknown unknowns can be gleaned by thinking about thinking; that is, the possibilities that might never have been considered. For example, during the 1962 Cuban missile crisis, when the United States and the Soviet Union were on the brink of a nuclear holocaust, US intelligence estimated that there were 6,000–8,000 Soviet troops on the island. This estimate was entirely logical (rational) because it was based on an analysis of the carrying capacity of Soviet ships arriving in port. It was also completely wrong. As Michael Dobbs says in his book, *One Minute to Midnight:*[5]

> *There was one missing element in these calculations: the ability of
> the Russian soldier to put up with conditions American soldiers
> would never tolerate.*

We now know that there were over 40,000 Soviet troops in Cuba. Almost all thinking is bounded by assumptions. If we can step back and try to identify those assumptions, it becomes easier to grasp the limits of our information.

Similarly, decision-makers should be wary of what seems to be rock-solid certain. For example, risks are frequently shaded red, amber or green. Red and amber typically attract most attention because they denote risks that have yet to be brought fully under control, whereas green usually means that appropriate mitigations are in place. When reviewing the risk register, busy decision-makers may well pass over the green risks month after month. Yet there is no law that requires firms to remain constant. Probabilities can change as people, hardware, software and so forth change. A risk brought under control at one time may have unravelled by another time.

Another possibility is to think differently. The discovery of BP's Thunder Horse field in 1999, containing 1 billion barrels of oil (one of the world's largest finds), happened because David Rainey, the company's head of exploration, encouraged his people to put geological data to one side and instead "think like a molecule of oil and where it might trickle to in the rock".[6]

Where possible, supplement regular information channels with softer, more intuitive ways of knowing. Bankers might lose less on bad loans if they actually met those seeking loans, as they used to, in order to assess whether they are a good risk, rather than simply relying on the data in the system.

Going into "lockdown"

There are two types of panic. One is where individuals rush around pointlessly, as if their hair were on fire. The other is where they freeze, for example by blocking the escape route on a burning aircraft, unable to move even to save themselves. Firms facing severe threats may also behave rigidly, going into corporate lockdown, when they:

■ restrict action to tried and tested routines;
■ restrict access to information;
■ restrict decision-making power to senior management.

When individuals are stressed they often revert to earliest-learned responses. For example, in response to tiredness, domestic airline pilots who trained on fighter aircraft may suddenly start to operate the controls as if they were flying fighter aircraft again.

Likewise, stressed firms may fall back upon well-learned responses and routines. As information flows up the hierarchy, the channels through which it must pass become more and more constricted. A severe threat may amplify this tendency: decision-makers may narrow the field of attention even further by drastically pruning the number of information channels used. Another indication of corporate lockdown is concentrating power and influence, whereby only those at the top are allowed to make decisions.

Going into lockdown can enable organisations to meet extreme situations. For example, when Lehman Brothers was tottering in September 2008, Merrill Lynch realised that unless it acted, it would be next to fall. Accordingly, it channelled all its efforts into negotiating a merger with Bank of America. A process that would normally take months was completed within days.

Yet these strictures can be self-defeating because they make firms less flexible in how they respond to threats. Moreover, because of the restricted flow of information and concentration of decision-making powers, the response may not be appropriate. For instance, firms may respond to a financial crisis by imposing blanket bans on staff recruitment and foreign travel and end up losing revenue when they most need it. A multinational company facing a cash flow problem insisted that all expenditure must have special authorisation. As a result, instead of dealing with the problem, the firm's general manager for Europe ended up signing chits for padded envelopes.

What is the question?

Another possibility is to change the line of questioning. For example, the risk of food contamination may reside not in the immediate suppliers, which are regularly vetted and inspected, but in the supply chains within the supply chains. Similarly, if a toy is deemed to be safe, instead of arguing about what the statistics mean, consider whether you would allow your own child to play with it. Then there are outliers. In science, the most important discoveries have sometimes come from studying exceptions and inconsistencies, like the milkmaids who never got smallpox. Similarly, the more important customer may be the one who did not buy. Effective decision-making is not just about questions. The art of decision-making lies in knowing the questions to ask.

Information-gathering must have a point

So far it has been suggested that decision-makers may be led astray by taking their information too seriously. Indeed, the only justification for the reams of reports and statistics that decision-makers habitually demand is if the marginal benefit derived from the information exceeds the marginal cost of collecting, collating and distributing it. Yet research suggests that much of a decision-maker's expensively collected information is either ignored or not considered until after the decision is made. What is the reason for this apparent paradox?

What is conspicuous is not so much the consumption of information as the insistence on possessing it. More specifically, decision-makers like to surround themselves with information because the process of gathering it, and appearing to analyse it and apply it systematically to decisions, enables them to demonstrate that appropriate attitudes to risk and uncertainty exist. Similarly, being first to have information, having more information than other people and/or having different information enables decision-makers to assert superiority. Most importantly, conspicuous possession of information makes decision-makers feel competent and in command of uncertainty.

The reality of planning

Planning can also impart an illusion of control. To be more precise, our reverence for rationality demands that decisions are supported by copious documentation couched in corporate language. For example, firms refer to "forward planning". But who ever plans backwards? Ideally, plans should be supported by pages and pages of econometrics and statistics. It does not matter if no one reads or understands the information, so long as there is plenty of it. A convincing plan is one that lands with a satisfying thud on decision-makers' desks.

Planning is alluring because uncertainty is officially abolished. Supporting statistics and econometrics help to banish doubt by lending projections an air of scientific authority. The language of planning completes the conquest. Phrases like "identify the main uncertainty drivers" imply that random events can be predicted and brought under control.

Yet planning is only dreaming with discipline. It can never be more than that because even the best researched plan is ultimately guesswork as projections cannot be verified. For instance, Tata Motors planned to sell at least 500,000 Nanos every year. Billed as "the people's car", the $2,000 Nano was to be the platform for the company's passenger-vehicle arm. So far, sales are barely one-fifth of the planned figure. Tata Motors missed one salient fact: few Indians want to own the world's cheapest car. It is called learning the hard way.

Moreover, the world for which we are planning is changing as we plan. This is why there is now has a worldwide glut of merchant ships. Industry forecasts depicting rising demand doubtless looked impressive. But the new fleets were ordered around 2005–06, well before the global financial crisis reversed the trend. Lesson: the gods laugh at those who make plans.

Even so, planning is important. What matters is not whether decisions went according to plan (they seldom do) but the quality of the planning. For example:

- Were important assumptions recognised and rigorously tested?
- If testing was not possible, were contingency plans adequate?
- Was progress properly monitored against the plan?
- Were adjustments to the plan made in a timely fashion?
- How appropriate were those adjustments?

In other words, the results are nearly always different from the plan. But they are usually better than if there is no plan at all. The main pitfall is overconfidence. Planning is alluring because it soothes our fears of the future, just as psychoanalysis soothes fears of the past. The important thing to remember is that uncertainty always lurks.

Ask why? not who?

Blame is a socially useful device. In times of crisis, assigning blame to individuals can help restore stability by making sense of untoward events and giving the impression that something is being done. Naming scapegoats deflects attention from other potentially culpable individuals. For example, when it emerged that Olympus, a maker of cameras and medical equipment, paid over $1 billion for worthless companies in order to hide losses on investments, three directors were sacked in an effort to suppress the scandal. Other Olympus directors may have known about the bogus companies. Assigning blame was an exercise in damage limitation.

The right question is not "who is to blame?" but "why did this happen?". For example, what may have changed in the firm or in the environment around the time that the problem developed? Changing suppliers can upset production processes even though, on paper, the new components are identical to those previously supplied. A minor change to software can create chaos if the change is not incorporated into desk instructions. Keep an open mind and keep asking "why?". The truth will eventually emerge.

5 Conspiracies of optimism: group dynamics

"How could we have been so stupid?"

John F. Kennedy

ST BENEDICT ENJOINS ABBOTS TO TAKE COUNSEL. His rules recognise that some decisions are too important to be left to individuals. Yet groups frequently make bad decisions. The World Health Organisation (WHO) works through a committee structure with elaborate checks and balances. Yet it seriously overestimated the probable death toll from SARS (severe acute respiratory syndrome) and swine flu. For instance, it advised countries to plan for a worst-case scenario of 7.5m deaths from swine flu. By mid-2010, the final death toll was below 18,000, compared with the normal global death toll of 500,000 from ordinary influenza. Countries that listened to the WHO ended up diverting huge sums of money from their health budgets to buy stocks of vaccine that were subsequently wasted. Similarly, the executive committee in charge of Tesco's billion-pound project to launch a chain in the United States named "Fresh and Easy" predicted that the venture would be in profit within two years. After six years of operation, Fresh and Easy had lost over £450m.

It is easy to understand why groups can fail. Bringing people together, giving them objectives and bidding them to work like a team regardless of body chemistry may not bring out the best in them. Moreover, almost all groups carry passengers. In a famous experiment, Max Ringelmann, a German psychologist, found that as more people joined a rope-pulling team, the average effort expended by individual team members fell. Indeed, studies of group behaviour reveal that most of the work in groups is done by a third of the membership.[1]

Conformity is another problem – and there is a paradox here. Without a measure of harmony and cohesion, a group is likely to splinter apart. Yet harmony and cohesion come at a price. This chapter explores why groups that seem to be working well as a team may make poor decisions. It also looks at what can be done to enhance group performance. But with any team, much depends upon the leader being able and willing to manage the group in a lively and provocative fashion.

Problems of status

Groups should make better decisions than individuals because they enable diverse knowledge, experience and mindsets to focus on a problem. Most importantly, groups exist to share information. Indeed, research has shown that the information groups share has an important influence on the final decision. Yet paradoxically, groups are often reluctant to introduce new information to the debate. They spend most of their time discussing what they already know.[2]

Status differentials are another block to information sharing and debate. Status divisions may be hierarchical, but can also arise informally. Theoretically, all members of a group may be equal. In practice, some are likely to be more equal than others. For instance, the marketing director may have higher status than the human resources director.

High-status members often dominate a group, sending and receiving more communications, and speaking more and commanding more attention and credence than lower-status members. But this does not mean they are always right. Moreover, since high-status group members often do most of the talking, lower-status members may find it hard to contribute to the discussion. If communication is blocked, decisions are not as well-informed as they could be. It would have been interesting, for example, to have observed the discussions that led up to Royal Bank of Scotland's decision to acquire ABN Amro in 2007. A consortium, led by the bank's former chief executive, Fred Goodwin, paid €71 billion (three times book value) for the Amsterdam-based bank – which according to analysts was already too expensive. The acquisition was Europe's biggest banking takeover, and it became one of the worst. By the time negotiations were completed, ABN Amro had already sold off the most valuable part of the business, the Chicago-based LaSalle unit, to Bank of America. Did Goodwin take counsel? Or was his status such that others were too much in awe of him to criticise the plan?

Impact of group culture

Cultural norms are informal codes of conduct that group members impose upon themselves. They apply to matters that are important to the group. For example, cultural norms may dictate who sits within eye contact of the leader, what subjects may not be discussed, whether dissent is tolerated and if so, how it is to be expressed. Conformity to cultural norms is the price of belonging to a group. Deviants risk sanctions and ultimately rejection.

The existence of cultural norms can help reduce friction, as group members do not need to decide the rules of the game every time they meet. Yet norms can be counterproductive if they inhibit discussion. Barings Bank's management group met every Monday. Polished courtesy distinguished the proceedings. Each director gave a brief verbal report on developments within their divisions. Cultural norms dictated that other members of the group listened politely. Rarely was there any discussion of those reports, far less any argument. In early February 1995, Peter Norris, head of investment banking, reported to the management group that Nick Leeson had made $9m "risk free" profit in one week. Diarmid Kelly, a director, observed, "You do not make $9m in a week with no risk."[3]

Kelly's remark should have triggered further enquiry. Instead, there was embarrassed silence. Andrew Tuckey, former deputy chairman of Barings, said afterwards:

> It was not our practice with senior colleagues to interrogate them as to what steps they had taken to bring themselves into a state of confidence and satisfaction ... Our culture was particularly inconsistent with that.

The culture of not interrogating group members meant that Barings lost one of the last chances to save the bank.

Groupthink: conspiracies of optimism

Poets and philosophers say that all things are generated by the mind and ask whether there is any escape from it. One thing groups are good at is making mindless decisions – a phenomenon known as groupthink. To be more precise, mind is a noun, like role, culture and system. It is not an object, like a brain, but a disposition to act in a certain way. To act mindfully is to concentrate, to think before acting. Whether the task involves baking a cake or appraising a multimillion-dollar project, the aim of engaging the mind is to achieve perfect performance. Acting mindfully differs from habit, which is when action is repeated. By contrast, when decision-makers act mindfully each performance is changed by the previous one as they learn from experience.

Membership of a group offers emotional warmth and psychological security in an uncertain and potentially hostile world. Groupthink refers to a lowering of analytical rigour as group members hesitate to challenge one another for fear of upsetting the cosy atmosphere. It results in "mindless" decision-making.

Symptoms of groupthink

- Self-serving explanations
- A sense of moral superiority
- Superficial analysis
- Stereotyping
- Self-censorship
- Pressure to conform
- An illusion of unanimous agreement
- The emergence of mind-guards and kitchen cabinets

When great minds think alike

Self-serving explanations

Few decisions go suddenly and completely awry. Calamity is usually foreshadowed by warnings. Rather than upset the cosy atmosphere by addressing those warnings, victims of groupthink resort to self-serving rationalisations. For instance, Enron's directors could hardly deny the falling share price. Yet instead of seeing the signal for what it was – that is, a long overdue reckoning – they said to one another: "It's not fair, the market doesn't understand us." Microsoft may have made a similar mistake over the launch of VISTA in 2007. Expectations (which Microsoft shared) were high. But the software was launched before it was fully tested. The result was widespread incompatibility and performance problems. Yet Microsoft seemed to believe that the $500m marketing campaign would somehow sweep the difficulties away. This self-serving belief only made things worse because it encouraged Apple and others to deride the product, leading consumers to think that VISTA had even more problems than it did.

A sense of moral superiority

Victims of groupthink see things in black and white. That is, they typically see themselves as "good" and outsiders as "bad". In other words, the group sees itself as inherently moral, incapable of acting unethically.

Outside hostility may amplify groupthink. The group offers psychological security, so members become all the more reluctant to upset one another. When Greenpeace activists boarded the derelict Brent Spar, Shell promptly sued for trespass and then fired water cannons at Greenpeace boats to prevent the activists reoccupying Brent Spar. Turning such hostility towards Greenpeace was a serious misjudgment. A protest that might have quietly fizzled out became a huge embarrassment for Shell. There were protests throughout Europe and uproar in the media. In Germany, Shell petrol stations were boycotted and vandalised. Eventually, the company was forced to abandon the Brent Spar disposal plan.

Superficial analysis

Victims of groupthink content themselves with superficial analysis. As subprime lending began to implode, UBS thought it was safe. It paid little attention to developments because all its subprime investments were AAA rated. Moreover, the fact that first-class paper was not affected strengthened the senior management's belief that the bank was impregnable. So when other banks began offloading positions regardless of credit rating, UBS was buying them up. It remained convinced that its subprime investments were secure – even though house prices were falling and it was becoming common knowledge that many subprime borrowers were struggling to repay their loans. Senior management should have thought more rigorously about the implications of developments at the lower end of the subprime market. Instead, they were complacent in the face of impending calamity.

Superficial analysis feeds overconfidence. For example, Tata Motors expected the Nano to be successful because it was so cheap (see Chapter 4). Positioned as a replacement for the scooters and motorbikes ubiquitous in rural India, and half the price of its nearest competitor, the Nano has most of the features of a basic car. Furthermore, the Ace, a small, inexpensive truck to replace three-wheeled rickshaws and a precursor to the Nano, was so successful that Tata had to build a new factory to cope with demand. But where was the extensive market research needed to test the all-important assumption that cheapness would guarantee huge sales? Unpleasant surprises happen because important issues are taken for granted.

Stereotyping

Stereotyping refers to an inappropriately fixed mental image. For instance, Western manufacturers were slow to recognise the competitive threat from Japan because the slogan "made in Japan" conjured up flimsy plastic toys and Datsun cars that rapidly rusted. Then firms such as Nissan and Honda signalled a change by offering consumers three-year warranties on new cars compared with the industry standard of one year. By the time Western companies realised that their perceptions of Japanese manufacturing were out of date,

Japan had stolen the lead. South Korean firms like Hyundai are now so sure of the quality of their vehicles that they are offering seven-year warranties on many of them. It is not clear how aware Japanese companies are of the emerging threat. The point is that stereotyped images can prevent firms from responding to weak signals in a timely fashion.

Self-censorship

Tesco's optimistic plan for its American Fresh and Easy venture contradicted a rule of thumb in the retail industry that it takes ten years to gain a foothold in a new country and another ten to build a brand. The members of the executive group were all highly experienced. Why did they guarantee failure by setting such an ambitious timescale? Possibly the group succumbed to self-censorship. That is, individuals may have suppressed their doubts or downplayed them in their own minds so as not to cause upset. Such collective mindlessness creates a false consensus. Since everyone seems to be in agreement, individuals may think that they are the only ones harbouring doubts. So they may well decide that they are overreacting.

No room for dissenters

If there is dissent, it is permitted only within socially prescribed limits. For instance, President Lyndon Johnson's advisory group, known as the Tuesday Cabinet, kept escalating the war in Vietnam despite clear evidence that the strategy was failing. The president habitually greeted a dissenter, Bill Moyers, with: "Well, here comes Mr Stop-the-Bombing." Tesco's equivalent would have been: "Well, here comes Mr Can't-do-it-in-Two-Years."

Incidentally, limited freedom of speech in a group may be worse than total suppression. This is because the group may think counter-arguments have been properly considered.

Living an illusion

Silence in the group is presumed to mean assent. As a false consensus emerges, disagreement becomes virtually unthinkable. This is because the illusion of unanimity bolsters members' self-esteem – that is, they start to believe that since everyone seems to be in agreement, the decision must be sound. The result is an illusion of control.

Rather than threaten members' self-esteem by asking awkward questions, or probing differences that might reveal disturbing issues and widely divergent assumptions, leaders emphasise similarities in the group's thinking. For example, a leader may say: "If you ignore X and Y, the consensus view of next year is quite close to where we think it should be." This is rather like saying: "If you ignore the abysmal sales figures, the new product launch is a success."

Mind-guards and kitchen cabinets

Another symptom of groupthink is the emergence of mind-guards. Mind-guards protect leaders from anyone who might shatter their complacency about the wisdom and morality of a proposed course of action. Leaders sometimes form inner circles. These so-called "kitchen cabinets" typically comprise small groups of close colleagues who can be trusted to agree with the leader on important matters. President Johnson's aforementioned Tuesday Cabinet invariably supported the policy of escalating the war in Vietnam. We may never know whether the three Olympus executives acted alone (see Chapter 4). They may have functioned as a kitchen cabinet, buttressing one another.

Often it is the leader who does most of the talking. This may not be healthy if it means that there is insufficient time for a full sharing of information. Appointing someone else to chair the group can help. Better still, the leader concentrates on listening and asking questions, not to make others feel inferior but to test the quality of the group's thinking. For example, how will expected gains be made? Have customers' needs been defined? What research has been done? How many sales people do we have? How many do competitors have? What alternatives have you considered? What customers do you plan to acquire? The purpose of such questioning is to prevent groupthink by inserting realism into the dialogue.

Consequences of groupthink

The main consequence of groupthink is a loss of analytical rigour, resulting in sloppy decision-making. More specifically, the group considers too few alternatives, perhaps only one or two obvious possibilities, rather than making the mental effort to generate more options. It is also reluctant to review initial decisions as more information becomes available and emotions change. The group may ask questions to give the appearance of rigour, but it avoids the hard ones. When Pepsi Raw, an expensive new drink made from natural ingredients, was launched in 2008, Pepsi hoped that "rum and Raw" might become an even more compelling combination than "rum and Coke". Two years later it was withdrawn from sale. Pepsi already had a "healthier" sugar-free product, Pepsi Max. What was the rationale for another? This was the hard question that Pepsi failed to address adequately.

When an organisation feels invulnerable, contingency planning seems superfluous. Consequently, when plans go awry, the organisation is taken by surprise. For instance, long before Greenpeace reacted, it is thought that other oil companies had privately remonstrated with Shell about the plan for Brent Spar, fearing a backlash against the whole industry. An overconfident Shell ignored those warnings.

Groupthink results in a conspiracy of optimism. But it is a silent conspiracy. Everyone in the group believes that everyone else must know what they are doing. Until events prove otherwise, that is.

Incidentally, conspiracies of gloom are also possible. For instance, research by psychologists has shown that if decision-makers have little appetite for risk, they are likely to see choices as more risky than they really are. Furthermore, the vividness trap mention in Chapter 2 can work in reverse: that is, if a dramatic but negative event occurs, decision-makers may see things as worse than they really are. If this happens they may be timorous when they need to be bold.

Risky shift

Groups are also prone to a phenomenon called risky shift, which occurs when a group selects an option that is riskier than the average preference. To be more precise, research by psychologists has shown that when individuals reach a provisional view on an issue, group discussion may lead them to take a more risky stance. Groups are also capable of cautious shifts.[4] In other words, group discussion often produces a shift towards the already preferred pole. For instance, in experiments where participants were invited to become judge and jury and were given evidence pointing to a defendant's innocence, group discussion made them more confident of their initial judgment. And they were more lenient in the recommended punishment. The reverse was also found. Where participants received evidence suggesting a defendant was guilty of an offence, group discussion polarised towards harsher pronouncements of guilt and harsher punishments.

Although hundreds of research studies conducted in many different countries have found evidence of polarisation, it does not always happen, or the shift may be fairly small. Yet the effects can be dramatic if the dominant members of a group favour more risky or more cautious options to begin with, as group discussion is likely to magnify those preferences. Committees often include people who sit together regularly. This makes them vulnerable to group pathologies. For example, WHO officials probably erred on the side of caution when first estimating the possible death toll from SARS. Group discussion may then have magnified fears of the virus mutating into a deadly strain, and produced an extremely cautious shift.

What causes risky and cautious shifts is a mystery. One theory is that since responsibility for failure is shared by the whole group, members feel more comfortable about moving to extremes. Mindsets may also be relevant. Research by psychologists has shown that defendants are treated more harshly when juries are composed of highly dogmatic individuals. In contrast, juries comprising less dogmatic individuals are more lenient. Furthermore, defendants who have similar attitudes to members of the jury typically receive more lenient treatment after group discussion. Where defendants have different attitudes from those of jurors, there is no shift. These experiments imply that some group decisions are almost a foregone conclusion, particularly when groups are composed of people with similar mindsets. As David Myers and Helmut Lamm say:[5]

The deliberation process might well be likened to what the developer does for an exposed film: it brings out the picture but the outcome is predetermined.

Groups and myopia

Like individuals, groups are prone to myopia. As the start date of the 2010 Commonwealth Games to be held in India approached, reports began to appear in the media that the village built to house the athletes was unfit for habitation. Then a crowded stand built by one of the many inexperienced contractors collapsed. Over 50 people were injured in front of a television audience of millions. Then there were reports of outbreaks of fever and typhoid caused by stagnant pools of water gathering in ruts left in poorly completed construction sites. Yet the organisers refused to believe there was a problem. Only when athletes began withdrawing from the competition was remedial work organised. Groups, like individuals, see what they want to see and hear what they want to hear.

Managing groups

There is little point in having a group discussion if members learn nothing new. Leaders can encourage group members to share information by identifying in advance the special knowledge and expertise possessed by individuals. Then the group can be primed to expect new information to be introduced into the discussion.

Where possible, group leaders should avoid sharp status divisions. It may be better to meet junior staff separately rather than having one meeting with everyone involved. Failing this, the leader should encourage participation by drawing out quiet people, listening generously and restraining the more voluble group members. It might be interesting to analyse a transcript of a discussion to see who dominates the group. Does the group follow the Pareto principle, whereby 20% of members speak for 80% of the time? Leaders should investigate why some members of the group keep quiet. They may have valuable contributions to make but have given up trying.

Often the leader does most of the talking, which may well mean that there is insufficient time for a proper exchange of views, ideas and information. Appointing someone else to chair a group can help. Even better is to have a leader who concentrates on listening and asking questions. A good example is President Kennedy's handling of the 1962 Cuban missile crisis, when the world faced a possible nuclear holocaust. The tapes of Kennedy's meetings with his advisers show that, far from dominating the proceedings, he spoke for less than 10% of the time. He also asked more questions than many other members of the group. This requires self-discipline and mental effort – the rewards come later.

Changing group culture

It is thought that almost all reasonably cohesive groups suffer from mild groupthink. Intelligence offers no protection. Diversity may reduce the risk of groupthink, but recruiting more women and more ethnic minority directors and non-executive directors will make little difference if recruits are all from similar social, educational, organisational or business backgrounds.

Cultural norms can persist for generations. Barings' gentlemanly code of conduct dated back to the bank's days as a partnership operating in a fairly staid environment. By 1995 the environment had become much more volatile and risky, so those norms outlived their usefulness.

A group imposes its own cultural code. Therefore only the group can change it. Yet leaders can pave the way for change. Studies of electronics firms and other high-tech organisations have shown that leaders can minimise tendencies to groupthink by stressing team-based values. These include valuing co-ordinated action rather than co-ordination of thought. They also imply a culture of mutual respect

---

Team-based values

- Receptive to new information, not just recycling familiar arguments
- Value diversity, not conformity
- Active listening and asking questions, not just waiting for a chance to interrupt
- Mutual respect, not following the party line
- Unity of action, not unity of thought

where members of the group are encouraged to disagree with one another, rather than adherence to the party line.[6] For example, a young research engineer employed by Hewlett-Packard said:

> The culture is very informal. I know that if I contradict the marketing man and say, "That's rubbish", I won't be punished for it.

In other words, leaders should be careful about making decisions that no one disagrees with.

Leaders can also encourage a group to review its performance. This exercise is usually best approached with the help of an independent facilitator, whose role is to guide the group towards committing itself to a new code of conduct.

Effective leadership

Leaders can promote mindfulness by encouraging group members to seek more nuanced information and make fine-grained interpretations rather than just accept reports at face value. They can also provoke members to doubt that which they are most sure of. For instance, President Kennedy kept reminding his executive committee not to rely on precedent in trying to predict how the Soviet Union would react to American intervention in Cuba. This time things might be different.

Open questions can be extremely effective in exposing poorly thought-out ideas. For example:

- What are you trying to achieve?
- How do you know you can achieve it?
- What will happen if you fail?
- Why are we doing this?
- What will happen if we do this?
- What will happen if we don't do this?

Leaders not only need to ask the right questions but must also judge whether the answers are adequate. Successful questioning is like peeling the layers off an onion:

- Where have you looked?

- Who have you asked?
- Why did you ask them?
- What did you ask them?
- What was the answer?
- How do they know?
- How far are you satisfied with the answer?
- Why?

The quotation "How could we have been so stupid?" refers to Kennedy's advisers' failure to anticipate the Bay of Pigs disaster. For instance, the military assured Kennedy's executive committee that in the unlikely event of the Bay of Pigs invasion failing, troops could shelter in caves. The group accepted this apparently reassuring information. But the caves were 80km from the beach, and troops would have to fight their way through jungle swamp to reach them. To have quizzed the military about the precise location of the caves would have endangered the esprit de corps that had developed in the group.

Behaving unpredictably can also help combat complacency. It is unsettling if group members are never sure what questions the leader will ask, or even where they are going to sit, far less what line they are going to take on a particular issue. Leaders should keep the group not just guessing, but guessing wrong.

As others see us

"*O wad some Pow'r the giftie gie us*
To see oursels as others see us!"

Robert Burns

Victims of groupthink lose touch with reality. Seeing ourselves as others see us is a powerful reality check. As Burns observed, such insight seldom comes naturally. Yet it can be cultivated. One possibility is to ask non-executive directors to meet outsiders. Do they share the board's perceptions of how well the company is performing and how it conducts itself?

Another approach is to consider the other party's point of

view. A good lawyer writes out the other side's case first. Likewise, good judgment means considering how an action might be seen by another party. This was Shell's mistake. It did not stop to think how others might view its Brent Spar plan. Similarly, Siemens had to reconsider its plan to become a major force in the atomic power industry in partnership with Russia's State Atomic Energy Corporation (Rosatom). The rethink was prompted by objections from employees. If Siemens had rigorously explored employees' reactions sooner, it might have spared itself the possibility of an embarrassing volte-face. Mont Blanc learned a similar lesson when it tried to market a special-edition fountain pen named after Mahatma Gandhi. It made only 241 pens, one for every mile Gandhi walked in 1930 on a protest march against a British salt tax. The decision became a public-relations embarrassment as protestors argued that the £16,000 pen was an insult to the memory of Gandhi, who stood for frugality and a rejection of the material world. Mont Blanc was surprised by the reaction as it had donated £90,000 to a charity run by the Gandhi family in order to obtain their approval. Yet it was forced to suspend sales and eventually withdraw the offending product. What matters is not how you see a decision, but how potentially hostile outsiders might view it.

Critical decisions require critical thinking

Times of crisis and high uncertainty amplify tendencies to groupthink. This is because a group's acute need for psychological security makes consensus all the more important. A premium on consensus means more pressure to conform. So when intellectual rigour is most needed, the group may be least able to exercise it. The right kind of leadership is therefore crucial.

Creating parallel groups to work on a problem can stimulate competition and thus improve analysis. Another option is to use sub-groups. Each group analyses one option in depth without the leader's presence or any knowledge of the leader's preferences. The whole group then meets to discuss the possibilities. President Kennedy used sub-groups effectively during the Cuban missile crisis. One group examined the possibility of an air strike to destroy the missile sites.

A second group examined the option of a naval blockade to prevent more weapons entering Cuba. Initially, the executive committee favoured an air attack, but it soon recognised that a blockade offered important advantages. It would be less provocative than a bombing raid and more effective, as bombers could easily miss their targets. It could be loosened or tightened as the situation developed, and it left open the option of an air strike. The decision-makers opted for a blockade. It is doubtful whether they would have done so without that detailed examination by a sub-group.

It may be useful to apply the so-called "nominal" technique whereby group members write down their ideas and publicise them before speaking. Allowing a private vote may help to reduce conformity. Introducing outsiders to a group can help sharpen the discussion. For instance, outsiders may pose new questions and suggest new insights. They can also prevent the group from becoming isolated.

As far as time permits, a group should guard against committing itself to a course of action too soon. Few decisions need to be made instantly. The group should give itself time to think, treating all ideas as tentative. These are then reconsidered as the discussion evolves and emotions cool. Members may also need time to consult their own departments to ensure that people with detailed knowledge and experience consider the proposals. Over time hidden possibilities may be revealed. For instance, when the WHO was urging countries to buy stocks of vaccine (see page oo), the Polish authorities took the time to make their own calculations. The result was that Poland was one of the few countries that did not waste money on superfluous stocks of vaccine. Moral: keep your head.

Refreshing the group

Long-established groups are most prone to groupthink because they develop habits. As time goes on, group interactions (the collective mind) become more routine and predictable. Members stop listening to one another because they have heard it all before. Even the most vibrant groups eventually lose their critical edge. For example, HTC, a Taiwanese telecommunications company, tried to avoid problems of groupthink by creating so called "magic labs" to drive research and development needed to produce cutting-edge smartphones and other products. The labs are staffed by people (known as wizards) from diverse and unconventional backgrounds, including jewellery design and computer animation, and are credited with many commercially successful innovations. Yet the fact that not all HTC's products have been spellbinding suggests that even wizardry becomes routine. Introducing new members can improve the quality of decisions because it disrupts the cosy pattern of interactions. The presence of new members also poses a new challenge.

Yet a need to belong is a powerful force. Lured by the prospect of cosy camaraderie, even new members, including the sharpest non-executives, may soon lose their critical edge. The most vibrant "tiger team" eventually softens.

The only people who do not experience the need to belong are loners – the people sometimes derided by psychologists as low on emotional intelligence. This is because they do not care what other people think of them. For instance, the president of a large Japanese real-estate firm hoped to persuade Steve Eisman, a financier, to invest. He sent Eisman his company's financial statements, which disclosed none of the important details about the company. Eisman lost patience. He waved the statements in the air and said, "This is toilet paper." Turning to the astonished interpreter, Eisman said, "Translate that."[7] Eisman may have displayed cultural insensitivity. He certainly overstepped the bounds of civilised discourse. Yet sometimes being rude is the only way to make an impression. The point is that groups may not like challengers – but they need them.

6 Shifting tides: power and politics in decision-making

"A camel is a horse designed by a committee."

Anon

THE LAUNCH OF APPLE'S IPAD was bad news for rival computer companies. One of the hardest hit was Microsoft, which a decade earlier had been the first to produce commercially viable tablet computers but had dropped the innovation because of fears that tablets would suck resources from mainstream products.

In theory, that should not happen. In theory, firms allocate resources to where they can do most good. Employees, moreover, do as they are told. But theory is a poor guide to what happens in practice. Firms do not always select the best, or economically wisest, course of action. Even if they do, it does not mean that decisions are always executed faithfully – or even executed at all.

This chapter explores how the shifting tides of internal power and politics can result in firms being pulled off course. The golden thread running through what follows is that although decision-makers may be in charge, they are not necessarily in control. Half the battle is recognising the fact. The other half is taking control – often without appearing to. It is known as triumph through not contending.

The dynamics of power

Decision-makers may issue directives. Employees may attempt to carry them out faithfully. Yet the results may not be as intended. To understand why firms get pulled off course, it is necessary to step back and consider what power is, and what it is not. Power is the ability to accomplish one's ends, regardless of resistance. Although people refer to "having power over" someone, power is not possession but a relationship. For instance, a gangster may have a gun (capability) and be willing to use it (intention). But without a victim, there is no power.

In other words, the exercise of power involves an exchange of influence between the power holder and the power target. That influence may be slight and fleeting but it is real nonetheless. And both parties are affected by it. For example, hostages sometimes end up identifying with their captors, and want to help them. Moreover, no one is completely powerless. No matter how asymmetrical the balance may be, the weaker party always has some control. A baby is completely dependent upon its parents. Yet when the baby cries, it is the parents who come running and the parents who arrange their lives around the baby's feeding times and other needs.

There is no such thing as absolute power matched by absolute subordination, no matter what appearances may suggest.[1] This is because even the most autocratic firm depends upon employees to execute orders. Dependency means that those who execute orders may have considerable discretionary power. Chief executives are said to be powerful because they command so many employees. Yet the more dependent people are on others the less power they have. For instance, in an interview by the *Financial Times* in July 2007, about a year before the global financial crisis erupted, Chuck Prince, former chief executive of Citigroup, said: "So long as the music is playing, you've got to get up and dance. We're still dancing." Although Prince's comments have been interpreted as a sign of collective myopia, they are ambiguous. He may also have been alluding to an industry-wide dilemma: that is, individual banks could forbid derivatives trading. But staff would feel frustrated and probably leave. In other words, Prince may have been alluding to the limits of his own power.

Dependency may also explain why some less than fully competent executives attain senior positions. These lightweights succeed because they are attentive to the emotional needs of more powerful people in the firm. They are typically the firm's "yes" men and women. By being solicitous, lightweights make more powerful people dependent upon them and are promoted as a reward for services rendered. It is called smile upwards and kick down.

Almost all power relations in firms involve dependency. Auditors are powerful but they depend on their clients to get the information they need to do their jobs. This means that they need co-operation from the audited organisation as it supplies the information. Moreover, auditors usually know less about the organisation they are auditing than those who work for it. They therefore have to check things with them or risk looking foolish. Checking enables the organisation to influence the auditors' report. For instance, it may argue that the auditors' recommendations are impractical; that the information is not readily available and too expensive to collect; that there are not enough staff to do the work that the auditors recommend; and so on. This is one reason Nick Leeson was able to conduct unauthorised trading with impunity. Resistance succeeds by manipulating the four deadly Ds: dilution, delay, dissimulation and deflection.

The problem with rules and instructions

Firms try to impose control by laying down rules. Yet control is never perfect. Rules do not apply themselves. Only people can do this. Even if employees attempt to apply the rules faithfully, the results may not be what the firm intended. This is because employees have to decide whether the rules apply in a particular case, what they apply to and how to apply them.[2] As people apply the rules differently, inconsistencies develop. Paradoxically, firms can be deflected simply by everyone following the rules, more or less. In other words, far from being rule bound, it may be more accurate to describe employees as making the rules as they go along.

Moreover, organisations cannot legislate for everything. Even the lowliest employee can acquire power informally through routine access to people, information and other resources.[3, 4] Although a secretary or a personal assistant may not be officially involved in the selection process for senior executives, they have the ear of the chairman or chief executive and can use this to express an opinion. This influence does not show on the organisation chart, but it is real nonetheless. It can even be decisive.

Ambiguity is another reason control is seldom perfect. Even the most precisely worded orders can be interpreted in different ways. For example, an instruction to close a factory immediately is ostensibly clear. Yet what does "immediately" mean? Does it mean this minute, or at the end of the working day or the working week? If so, what about work in progress? Or does it mean accept no more new contracts, in which case it might be six months or a year before production finally ceases? Similarly, what exactly constitutes a reportable accident? Ambiguity enables employees to include their own ideas about what should be done. And these ideas may not be what decision-makers intend.

Low power

Seniority confers power that is wide in scope but low in intensity. Chief executives are responsible for many things. But because their power is so wide, their ability to exert control over any one issue is correspondingly low. Conversely, those at lower levels may control only a few things, but as a result their grip is considerable. One of the earliest examples of such intense power concerns the Imperial Chinese civil service, which was run by clerks who used their mastery of detail to frustrate their superiors (much like the British civil service). For example, multiple copies of all reports, records and other communications were required. Each type of document had its own prescribed style. No deviations were allowed.

A more modern example of the difference between scope and intensity of power is Chuck House, a young engineer employed by Hewlett-Packard, who made a bid to supply an improved airport control tower monitor to the Federal Aviation Authority (FAA). It failed because the model did not meet the FAA's requirements for a high-resolution picture. Even so, as his design was smaller, lighter, brighter and more energy efficient than the competition, House persevered. Without authority, he conducted market research. He also broke a company rule forbidding the showing of prototypes to customers.

HP's marketing people tried to kill the project. They claimed that the demand for monitors was minuscule. House argued that they had only contacted existing customers, whereas new technology meant new uses and therefore new customers. Even so, marketing won. There would be no more resources for House's oscilloscope technology. David Packard, co-founder of HP, said: "When I come back next year I don't want to see that project in the lab!"

Covertly supported by his line manager, House quietly shuffled budgets and developed the project. He aimed to move it into production within a year instead of the normal two years to comply with Packard's instruction to remove it from the laboratory. The result was eventually an oscilloscope for the moon mission, a medical monitor used in the first heart transplant and a prize-winning large-screen oscilloscope for special events. Packard was powerful but too busy to check up on House. House had little power but used his access to laboratory resources, budgets and so on to frustrate his hierarchical superior – though with happier results than in the ancient Chinese civil service.

Inevitable tensions

Without co-operation there would be no organisation. Yet co-operation usually co-exists with conflict. HTC began life in 1997 as a contract manufacturer making PDAs (personal digital assistants) for other firms. In 2006, it made the risky but ultimately successful decision to start branding phones under its own label. Shareholders were doubtful, even hostile to the proposal. Peter Chou, HTC's chairman, had to work hard to convince them. The shareholders' doubts were well founded. For example, it took Audi many years to become regarded as a global brand in its own right rather than a mere offshoot of VW. Moreover, creating a brand meant HTC would have to assume inventory, marketing, support and warranty risks, as well as the possibility of a conflict of interest. Moreover, not all Taiwanese contract manufacturers had made the transition successfully. When Acer started manufacturing products under its own name it began to lose contract orders. The company ended up having to spin off its contract business into a new company called Winstron. BenQ lost $700m trying to build a global brand. Even though Siemens paid BenQ more than $300m to relieve it of its loss-making mobile-phone business (see page 10), BenQ filed for bankruptcy just a year later, having lost $700m in the venture. Why should HTC be different?

In June 2009, Giancarlo Di Risio resigned as chief executive of Versace, prompted by a clash with the label's creative director, Donatella Versace. Given the economic downturn and the company's precarious financial position, Di Risio wanted to cut back on spending. Versace disagreed. She considered it important to continue spending on lavish parties and other forms of promotion. Uncertainty is one reason conflict exists. If everyone knew what was best for an organisation all the time, there would be less to argue about.

The trouble is that everyone thinks they know. Engineers want to build products that embody engineering excellence. As they see it, competitive advantage lies in being first to offer new features. Accountants are more interested in payback periods, return on investment and capital requirements. Since engineers and finance people look at the same project from different angles, they may well reach different conclusions about whether it should go ahead. Moreover, these conclusions may be diametrically opposed.

Scarcity also creates tension. Someone has to decide who in the firm gets what, where, when and how. Which depot gets the new buses first? Should the company spend more on advertising and less on training? Which projects are to be culled? Vested interests naturally try to influence those decisions. The three main ways in which influence is exerted are through control of the:[5]

- basis on which the decision is to be made;
- alternatives that are considered;
- information there is about alternatives.

Chapter 3 shows how problem definition shapes subsequent action. Those who are able to shape the issues can have a powerful hold over outcomes. Another tactic is controlling what alternatives are placed before decision-makers. For example, a study of venture capitalists found that funding decisions were often made outside the formal arena.[6] Venture capitalists quietly formed alliances and agreed to support funding for others' pet projects, provided the favour was reciprocated. Less-favoured projects were not even considered. Similarly, a landmark study of internal politics at ICI, a British chemical company taken over in 2008 by AkzoNobel, a

Dutch conglomerate, found that an employee succeeded in getting his choice of computer accepted by acting as a gatekeeper. He controlled information about alternatives by making sure that information about his preferred model was always put before decision-makers first. He also mentioned the name of his preferred computer more frequently and more enthusiastically than other models.[7] Such tactics can be hard to spot and even harder to control.

The politics of the deadly Ds

A decision changes nothing. Someone has to implement it. The four deadly Ds referred to earlier – of delay, deflection, dilution and dissimulation – are classic tactics for stopping an unpopular decision. Employees know that if they simply do nothing, decisions are often forgotten. More subtly, a decision gets referred for further analysis. A working party is set up to work out the details. By the time it reports, the decision may well have been overtaken by events. Delay works because it usually results in one party becoming weaker and the other stronger.

Thinking the unthinkable

The highest form of power in any organisation is invisible. It resides in the status quo, the issues that are never discussed and the taken-for-granted assumptions about what is appropriate. In other words, real power is silent. This power means that although resources sometimes accrue to those who shout loudest, the most powerful people in the firm are those who never need to shout because of seemingly unchallengeable assumptions about an organisation. They receive resources automatically. For instance, at Hewlett-Packard R&D was sacrosanct. When Mark Hurd became chief executive in 2005, he cut the number of research projects from about 150 (including many small ones) to 20–30 major endeavours. He also put more emphasis on technology transfer and on cutting development times. Such interference in R&D was unprecedented, and until then unthinkable.

Why should such intervention be unthinkable? (Even Hurd felt obliged to stress that he was not cutting budgets, only redirecting resources for research.) In theory, the balance of power in organisations reflects operational needs. For instance, during the early "smokestack" era, keeping production lines moving was all-important, so chief executives were often engineers. During the 1920s and 1930s, selling goods and services became more important than producing them, so chief executives typically had sales or marketing backgrounds. By the 1970s and 1980s, shareholder value and relationships with the financial community assumed centre stage, so chief executives were drawn more from accounting and finance.

In practice, organisational change lags behind change in the operating environment. Moreover, when critical uncertainties change, powerful people may be reluctant to step down and make way for those with the requisite expertise. Organisations ruled by legacy seldom shine. For instance, until the arrival of Peter Löscher, Siemens was run by engineers who were interested more in technical excellence than whether products made commercial sense.

The art of the possible: managing power and politics

Managing power and politics is the art of the possible. Regardless of what management pundits may say about executives "blasting their way through obstacles", decision-makers are more likely to succeed if they go round them.

As the aphorism goes, "to get on, go along". Oblique approaches can be more successful than direct confrontation. It is better to offer a new idea as an additional possibility than to present it as a competing option. This softer tactic of adding rather than supplanting is less likely to spark resistance. For example, instead of confronting a militantly led trade union, it may be wiser to take an indirect approach by encouraging the growth of a second, rival union during a period of unrest, as happened in the UK coal industry in the 1980s. Another approach might be to promote militant officials to supervisory and managerial positions. In short, triumph through not contending.

The art of the possible does not mean giving in. It means recognising that other people in the firm have goals that are important to them. They are much more likely co-operate if, by doing so, they can achieve their goals. Between 2357 and 2205 BC, China suffered devastating seasonal floods. Dykes were built to contain the rivers, to no avail. The river invariably burst its banks and flooded the rice fields. A different approach was tried. King Yu of the Hsia dynasty ordered the rivers to be dredged and channelled. The flooding stopped because these measures enabled the river to reach its goal – the sea – more easily. Burger King's decision to sell hamburgers for 99 cents and McDonald's decision to improve restaurants despite the downturn (see Chapter 7) had opposing effects. McDonald's found that the refurbishments meant higher profits, which enabled franchise-holders to achieve their goal of making money. Burger King's policy resulted in the opposite and so provoked acrimony.

The art of the possible also involves seeking to change the balance of power by lowering the other party's expectations, by mentioning that another buyer is interested, by signalling that you are in no hurry to reach an agreement, and so on. In power relations there is always a counter ploy.

Getting the approach right

It may be tempting to seize problems by the scruff of the neck and force a decision. But unless urgent action is needed, this may not be wise. Time allows people to exhaust themselves in argument. Once they are exhausted, it is easier to steer them. At the very least, no one can claim that they were not consulted. Nor is it wise to announce that you have found a solution. It is better to let others grapple with a problem and guide them towards finding a solution for themselves. They are then more likely to be committed to implementing it.

Taking one's time does not necessarily mean being slow. It means allowing things to take their course. For instance, rather than tell someone that they are wrong, it is better to ask them to explain why they think they are right. Similarly, if two executives clash over what should be done, it might be better to give them time to reach an agreement between themselves, rather than to impose a decision. Imposition is a last resort if they cannot agree.

Neither does allowing time necessarily mean being passive. It allows for ideas and assertions to be probed and areas of agreement as well as difference to be identified. Asking questions is the best way to enable people to see the flaws in their ideas for themselves. This saves having to point them out. Diplomacy is the art of letting people have your way.[8]

In Western society, we are taught to find the "right" answer. This approach conditions us to believe that there is only one right answer to a problem. In this view, if one solution is right, all other solutions must be "wrong". Western education also stresses the negative rather than the positive. For example, examination questions prefaced "critically analyse", "critically discuss" or "critically evaluate" encourage us to think about what is wrong with an idea. In business decision-making, there may be more to be gained by thinking how ideas may be useful and how opposing ideas may be creatively combined. Conflict resolution need not always mean making winners and losers.[9]

Similarly, Western societies like clarity and the intuitive reaction to any ambiguity is to add detail in, for example, specifications and instructions. Yet that may only cause worse confusion. A better approach may be to specify a few important parameters and then allow discretion to be used. For instance, when Honda designed the Box Car, engineers were given only three parameters: it must be small, energy efficient and sell well. It did. Less is often more.

Managing conflict

Healthy debate untarnished by internal politics is something all organisations should aspire to. But conflict and destructive politics are inevitable. Decision-makers must manage them otherwise they will manage the decision-makers. Aristotle saw politics as a means of creating stability amid diversity – hence the notion of *polis* as a gathering together of many members. Politics works by reconciling competing interests and different ideas. The aim is to create a reasonably stable social order without resorting to dictatorship and coercion.

The starting point is recognising that there are two types of disagreement. Substantive disagreement refers to the different views about issues such as future prospects, the merits of new technology, the superiority of one engineering technique over another, the best packaging design and so forth. This is healthy and should be encouraged, up to a point. The second type of conflict relates to interpersonal tensions and infighting between individuals and rival factions. This is unhealthy and should not be tolerated.

Yet even healthy conflict has to be managed. If not, it could turn into unhealthy conflict. This means getting everyone to agree on the rules of the game. For instance, what etiquette is to be observed when expressing disagreement?

The best way of dealing with factions and infighting may be to engineer matters so that protagonists have to work together. This might be achieved by creating sub-groups of people who have competing interests and who would not normally work together; or by getting executives to research and advocate a different position – perhaps one that they have previously been opposed to. Another tactic for managing conflict is to ensure that no one has complete information. Then people must listen to one another. In short, divide and rule – but do this constructively.

Knowing when not to fight is as important as knowing how to fight. Fighting is only worthwhile if a really important issue is at stake – for example, if winning could create change of lasting value. Similarly, rather than becoming caught up in debilitating debate, it may be worth making small concessions and fudges just to keep the peace. Always consider the alternative, to compromise, which may be worse.

Getting people to raise their game is integral to reducing conflict and lifting performance. When the Campbell Soup Company faced falling sales, the management team concentrated on who was to blame – and compounded the problem by cutting costs and even taking the chicken out of the soup. The first thing a new chief executive, Doug Conant, did was to raise the level of the debate, encouraging the management team to redefine the brand mission to the nobler aim of nourishing people. His next move was to ask executives to work on a new strategy – a task that took them beyond their own departments. Such game-raising aspirations are one of the best ways for decision-makers to rise above the pettier forms of politicking.

Ending the debate

Patience may be a virtue, but dilatoriness is not. The UK authorities were accused of dilatoriness in their response to BSE (bovine spongiform encephalopathy or "mad cow disease" as it is popularly known). For ten years the official view was that it was unlikely that BSE posed any risk to humans and that beef was safe to eat. According to the official inquiry, over 170,000 animals died or were slaughtered as a precaution, and so far the death toll from the human variant, Creutzfeld-Jacob disease (CJD) is though to be at least 80 people in the UK, most of them young.

Consultation and discussion should be limited to what the situation affords. If decision-makers do not have the luxury of time, shortened debate is better than none at all. Or they could explain that there was no time to consult. As long as it does not happen too often, people will understand.

Striving for consensus risks any of those involved choosing to exercise a veto. What matters is ensuring that people have had the opportunity to express an opinion. Whether they agree with the decision is beside the point. It is also unwise to underestimate resistance. The most entrenched executives are usually those who profit most from the status quo. For example, James Dyson invented a new type of vacuum cleaner that would make a fortune. If Hoover had invented such a machine, it might well have gone the way of Microsoft's tablet computer. Just as turkeys never vote for Christmas, the old order will never support change if it feels threatened. For instance, Microsoft also invented ClearType, a technology that improved screen reading. Other groups in Microsoft felt threatened by the new invention, so they did their utmost to discredit it:[10]

Engineers in the Windows group falsely claimed it made the display go haywire when certain colors were used. The head of Office products said it was fuzzy and gave him headaches. The vice president for pocket devices was blunter: he'd support ClearType and use it, but only if I transferred the program and the programmers to his control.

Rather than become involved in endless arguments, and be pulled this way and that by powerful factions, it may be better to announce a decision. Politics feeds off uncertainty. If decisions are cut and dried, there is nothing to resist. Except implementing them, that is. Autocracy works best if others are allowed to shape the details. For instance, marketing people may lose 20% of their budget. The decision is non-negotiable, but they are allowed to shuffle funds between accounts in order to achieve the shortfall. In other words, always leave the other party with their self-esteem.

The importance of authority

Chaos exists in the gap between the old order vanishing and the new one emerging. Decision-makers should try to minimise that gap. For instance, when Peter Löscher took charge at Siemens half the operational management team were dismissed. The old committee structure was swept away and replaced by a system of individual accountability. Radical though these changes were, Siemens was not seriously destabilised because they were made swiftly and decisively. Swiftness leaves no room for rumours and conspiracy theories to flourish. Decisiveness means people know where they are. As Löscher recognised, people worried about paying the mortgage seldom perform well. The last thing that Siemens needed was a lot of poor performers. When leaders are decisive, people may not like their decisions, but at least they know where they stand and can plan. Autocracy is better than indecision.

New policies must be supported by deeds as well as words. One of the most important and fragile controls in organisations is authority. Although we may speak of authority figures and people in authority, authority only really exists as a quality of a relationship. If one party to a relationship is allowed to ride roughshod over the needs of another party, authority is destroyed. For example, when compliance officers are publicly derided by senior traders, or engineers are bullied into certifying something as safe against their better judgment, authority fails. Authority stands or falls upon respect for another's needs. It is a culture that decision-makers do well to instil. The alternative is anarchy.

Missing links

To exercise judgment, decision-makers have to rely upon information supplied by others. When supplying information, people naturally try to present themselves in a good light. This can mean being creative with the truth. For example, projects are almost always "virtually finished" and "on schedule" and "on budget". Either that, or there is always a plausible excuse. When examining those claims, there are three important questions:

- What might have been left out?
- What might this person know that I would be interested to know too?
- What am I not hearing?

One example of what can happen when decision-makers fail to ask the right questions is the Nimrod disaster. A Nimrod aircraft flying on a routine mission over Afghanistan in 2006 exploded in mid-air, killing all 14 personnel. The immediate cause of the explosion was leaking fuel igniting. The leak was caused by an engineering flaw inherent in the aircraft's design, but as it was hidden behind pipes and ducting it was not noticed during routine maintenance. The main chance of discovery was when the Nimrod Safety Case (meant to find and fix potential hazards before they cause an accident) was compiled by BAE Systems, acting on behalf of the Ministry of Defence Nimrod Project Team. QinetiQ acted as independent advisers to the project team. The Safety Case should have involved an exhaustive examination of the aircraft. The official enquiry into the disaster, however, describes it as poor, undermined by the belief that Nimrod was "safe anyway" because it had flown for over 30 years. It was a "box-ticking" exercise, puffed up by copious documentation to give the impression that a huge amount of work had been done. However, many hazards were left "open" or "unclassified" or referred for "further work". The Safety Case was presented and signed off at a Customer Acceptance Conference. Although it listed hazards that had not been addressed and other outstanding work, the Nimrod project team failed to probe these in sufficient detail. Instead, it "succumbed to pressure to be party to a 'consensus' that the Safety Case was complete". Although QinetiQ should have drawn attention to these omissions, it was allegedly "too compliant and eager to please ... having already been briefed not to expect any problems". A QinetiQ employee said:[11]

> The customer didn't want problems. That was quite clear, and that was made abundantly clear to me. "Take that out, the customer doesn't want to hear that."

The Safety Case took four years to complete. The Customer Acceptance Conference lasted two days. The aircraft was destroyed in six minutes. When the Nimrod project team and QinetiQ listened to the BAE Systems presentation, they were told what work had been done. What they were not hearing much about was all the issues that had been marked in the Safety Case as "open" or "unclassified" or referred for "further work". The art of decision-making may lie in knowing the questions to ask. But decision-makers still have to ask.

The old, old story

Apparent consensus may reflect groupthink (see Chapter 5), but it may equally reflect the politically adroit sense among some people as to which way the wind is blowing. Those people know there is more to be gained by acquiescence than by opposition. According to Machiavelli, others will say what they really think only if they can be sure that honesty will not offend. Even then, people have their own careers and other interests to consider. Dean Rusk, an American secretary of state in the 1960s, had a formula for survival:[12]

> To endure and survive, to keep playing a mediocre hand rather than risk all for a better one, and to stand around for greater achievement another day.

Decision-makers should remember that those around them also practise the art of the possible. Moreover, they may be extremely good at it.

7 Predictable surprises

"Next to a battle lost, the greatest misery is a battle gained."
Duke of Wellington

IN 1374 KATHERINE DUCHEWOMAN, who "wrought up the loom ... false work" made "of linen thread but covered with wool ... against the ordinances the trade", had her cloth ("4 yards in length and 7 quarters in breadth") burned before her eyes. John Penrose, having sold wine "'unsound and unwholesome for man' was forced to drink a draught of the same and have the remainder poured over his head".[1]

The medieval guilds of Europe were extremely powerful. Anyone wishing to work as a craftsman had to invest all their assets in the guild; membership was for life and involved the whole family. Moreover, as the unfortunate Duchewoman and Penrose discovered, the penalties for infringement were harsh.

The factory system was anathema to the guilds. Yet their implacable opposition could not halt the advent of mass production. The new captains of industry did not waste time arguing with the guilds. They simply circumnavigated them. As the Industrial Revolution progressed, these once omnipotent organisations died or became charities – for example, the Worshipful Company of Tallow Chandlers and the Worshipful Company of Cordwainers and other livery companies of the City of London. But if the guilds had worked with the Industrial Revolution instead of against it, they might have had some influence on events.

Europe's medieval monasteries were organised in a highly efficient manner. Monks practised specialisation (basketry, weaving, brewing and so forth) and division of labour centuries before the advent of the factory system. The monks understood logistics, estate management and job rotation. They compiled work instructions and manuals centuries before "total quality management". Their efficiency made them extremely wealthy. Yet that wealth became their undoing, as the monks became lazy and self-indulgent.

All decisions have some unintended consequences, but sometimes these are the opposite of what the decision-makers intend. In trying to preserve their power, the guilds lost it. Similarly, the monasteries used management techniques to maximise the time available for prayer and other devotional activities. They became too successful for their own good. So far this book has focused on why individuals and firms sometimes exercise poor judgment. This chapter looks at the opposite problem. It explores how decision-makers can act in ways that seem rational and purposeful yet prove self-defeating. Such "predictable surprises" can be avoided by developing an eye for paradox and in particular by recognising that it is possible to have too much of a good thing.

Today's solution: tomorrow's problem

We expect solutions to remove problems. Yet solutions all too often create new problems. When concerns about healthy eating caused business to stall in the late 1990s, McDonald's diversified, buying various restaurant businesses. The strategy simply created more problems because McDonald's management became hopelessly overstretched. Burger King's aforementioned (see page 93) decision to introduce the 99 cents hamburger to stimulate business in the wake of the global financial crisis was a runaway success in that customers flocked in to buy bargain burgers. Unfortunately, fewer people than usual bought the more expensive (profitable) items on the menu, leading to acrimonious disputes with franchisees, as their profits disappeared. Similarly, Continental, a tyremaker, sought to reduce the risk of being dependent on one sector by diversifying into others. Yet Continental's tyre business ended up supporting the new ventures. Tablet computing has brought us as close to the notion of the paperless office as we are ever likely to get, as people no longer need to carry papers with them to meetings. The danger is that because printing costs no longer apply, documents get longer. Yesterday's solution becomes today's problem.

Sometimes the solution is the problem. On May 6th 2010, Wall Street experienced a sudden shock when the price of many American equities suddenly and inexplicably plummeted and then rapidly recovered. About 20,000 trades in over 300 securities were executed by automated systems at prices 60% away from what they had been just seconds earlier. Within 20 minutes, $1,000 billion had been wiped off the value of American shares. Procter & Gamble's share price fell by 35%, and Accenture's dropped from $40 to 1 cent. Shocked traders thought that a European bank was about to fail.

Twenty minutes later the market was back to normal and trades where the movement was more than 60% were cancelled. A subsequent investigation concluded that the "flash crash" was caused by a rapidly executed $4.1 billion sale of stock index futures by a single institutional investor on a day when the atmosphere was already tense. That is, instead of using an intermediary to execute such a large trade, or making a series of sell orders on its own account, the institution selected an automated execution logarithm without regard to price or time. The automated execution of this "sell" program triggered a wave of rapid buying and then selling by arbitrageurs creating a "hot potato" effect. There have since been other flash crashes in the sugar and cocoa markets, thought to have been caused by high-frequency traders who hold securities sometimes only for a few seconds. Automated trading systems were a solution to speeding up business. The solution works but at the expense of creating new and unforeseen problems.

Solutions that work in the short term can make things worse in the longer term. Shipping companies that quietly pay the ransom demands of Somali pirates solve the immediate problem of getting valuable cargo released. In the longer term, it just provides an incentive for piracy. It also gives the pirates more money to make themselves more effective – they become super-pirates. In other words, the solution not only reproduces the problem, it also amplifies it.

When solutions dictate or distract

In theory, decision-making starts with a problem. Having analysed the problem, decision-makers then select a solution. In practice, it is often the other way round. Firms are populated with solutions looking for problems to attach themselves to:[2]

> A solution is somebody's product. A computer is not just a solution to a problem in payroll management, discovered when needed, it is an answer actively looking for a question ... Despite the dictum that you cannot find the answer until you have formulated the question well, you often do not know what the question is ... until you know the answer ... Every entrance is an exit.

When solutions latch onto problems, the result may be a subtle shift between master and servant. For instance, presentations become tailored to what PowerPoint can handle. Moreover, because PowerPoint offers so many different options, presenters may devote more time to thinking about the form of the presentation than the substance. Instead of using specialist software to test their ideas, textile designers may use it to generate ideas. Consequently, their designs may lack originality because they merely reflect the confines of the software. Similarly, a scientist says:

> When I started out [as a scientist] computers were the size of the room so we could only use them to check our calculations. Now that computers are a lot smaller and a lot more powerful, scientists use them to trawl their data instead of thinking about what they are looking for. There are some scientists who do the deep thinking first. They get superb results.

Similarly, risk management becomes reduced to managing the risk register. Performance management becomes reduced to managing scorecards. Thus many solutions subtly deflect firms, as activities that are a means to an end become the end themselves.

A drunk looks for his car keys not where he dropped them but under a street lamp because the light happens to be good. Organisations sometimes behave in a similar fashion. For instance, Bernard Madoff's $65 billion Ponzi scheme was finally exposed in 2008 after he confessed to his sons. It could have been discovered years earlier as there were numerous complaints to the authorities concerning his improbably consistent returns. Yet the authorities focused their investigations mainly on the possibility of insider trading. Asked why other complaints were not investigated, an official said that he focused on insider trading because "that was the area of expertise for my crew".

In other words, if all we possess is a hammer, every problem becomes a nail.

Winner's curse

"I won the auction but don't want the prize" is the title of a paper exploring the winner's curse.[3] The term "winner's curse" was first coined when the American government auctioned licences to drill for oil. Economists reasoned that providing all bidders shared the same information, they would all bid the same price. However, there was considerable variance. Moreover, the highest bids were usually from companies employing incompetent geologists who overestimated the level of reserves being offered for sale. This discovery led economists to predict that winners would probably be "cursed" when bidding for items of uncertain value. That is, the winners would probably be bidders who overestimated the value of those items rather than bidders who underestimated their value.

Firms frequently have to compete for resources. Winning can become a curse if firms pay so much that they cripple themselves financially and are unable to exploit their expensively won prize. Almost any competition can result in winner's curse. Contractors may underprice bids to win work only to discover that their bid is so low that they are unable to complete the work and end up defaulting on the contract. When it comes to new share issues, investors are inevitably "cursed". If the issue is popular, they receive fewer shares than they applied for. If the issue is unpopular, they get their full allocation but the shares go down in price when trading in them starts. A famous example of winner's curse is the auction in 2000-02 by European countries of 3G mobile telephone licences. The media called it the most expensive game of poker in history as bidders vied with one another, each trying to guess how the other would bid. Mathematicians were employed to calculate how much rivals would be prepared pay and to predict the precise conditions under which they would or would not bid. Yet the victors paid so heavily for their licences that they could no longer afford the necessary research and development. They ended up surrendering their licences to the government. History repeated itself on a smaller scale just a year later as Dutch radio stations overbid for radio frequency. Lesson: be careful what you wish for.

The winner's curse is a form of myopia. Bidders become so intent on winning the prize that they fail to consider the implications of bidding higher than anyone else, while having the same information disadvantage relative to the seller as every other buyer. This is why they end up overpaying. Ratan Tata, chairman of Tata Steel, an Indian steelmaker, was reported to be overjoyed when he finally wrested Corus, an Anglo-Dutch steelmaker, from rival bidder CSN, a Brazilian steelmaker. Yet the media predicted that joy would be short-lived. Not only was the £6.7 billion purchase price a third more than Corus's board originally agreed as a fair price for the company, but Tata also borrowed heavily to finance the acquisition – a dangerous gamble in a volatile industry. The media accused Tata of trying to keep up with the Joneses, or rather the Mittals, in striving to become one of the world's top five steel producers. Indeed, in 2010, Tata was forced to mothball (and subsequently close) its Teesside plant in the UK, putting 1,700 jobs at risk and provoking the epitaph in the media, "rust in peace". Tata could have protected himself against overpaying simply by adjusting downwards his estimates of what the acquisition was worth.

The curse of establishment status

In the 1950s the City of London was very different from the fiercely competitive workaholic culture that we know today. Brokers wore bowler hats. As a mark of their status, government brokers wore top hats. As late as 1981, it was the duty of the deputy governor of the Bank of England to drop a penny into the upturned "toppers" while their owners were closeted with the governor on their daily visits to the bank. Directorial hours were 10am to 3pm, including a long lunch preceded by a dry sherry in the partners' room.

The catalyst for change was Sigmund Warburg, who fled from Nazi Germany and founded, with Henry Grunfeld, S.G. Warburg & Co in 1946. Warburg's dynamism provoked a hostile response from the old order. In a rare interview given late in life, Warburg said:[4]

I remember some people in very good houses talked very nastily behind my back: "Do you know this fellow Sigmund Warburg? He starts at the office at eight o'clock in the morning". This was considered contemptible ... They looked down upon me with the utmost snobbism.

Nicknamed a financial Rasputin, Warburg helped develop the Eurobond trade and led the City's first hostile takeover. Eventually antagonism subsided and he received a knighthood. Even so, he remained cautious. He thought that the worst thing that could happen to the bank would be to become part of the City establishment. Establishment status, he said, creates a temptation to become lazy, self-satisfied and complacent. Yet Warburg probably understood the advantages too. Establishment status implies trust. Trust speeds up the conduct of business because it enables parties to take mutually beneficial shortcuts such as verbal contracts knowing that the other party will honour them subsequently, hence the motto *dictum meum pactum* (my word is my bond).

Trust can also mean favourable treatment. For instance, research has shown that establishment firms are more likely to be granted bank loans than outsiders. They also generally pay less interest. Yet as Warburg shrewdly observed, establishment status can become a curse. A study of entrepreneurial clothing companies in the United States found that establishment firms become less efficient because they become too insular; they are forever granting and returning favours to one another rather than optimising their resources. Moreover, easy access to loans and other resources can mean that firms eventually stop looking outside the network so they may miss better possibilities. Establishment firms also tend to have poor shock absorbers. If one firm in the network supplying other network firms is suddenly bought out, the others may suffer because they have no immediate alternative. Paradoxically, the very social inclusion that new firms strive to achieve may eventually dissipate their entrepreneurial zeal.

The tragedy of the commons

Two people were sharing a tent. A tiger suddenly appeared. The first person grabbed his shoes and started to run. "It's no good," said the second person. "You'll never outrun the tiger." "I don't need to outrun the tiger," said the first person. "I only need to outrun you." In fact, the tiger ate them both. Yet if they had helped one another to escape, perhaps by climbing a tree, both might have survived.

This story shows how the pursuit of individual interest can spell collective ruin. The notion was exemplified in a famous essay published in 1968 by Garrett Hardin, entitled "The tragedy of the commons".[5] The commons were tracts of land where every peasant was entitled to graze animals free of charge. Since every peasant used the facility, the land became overgrazed and was ruined.

Many social and economic problems reflect the dynamics of the commons. Firms can profit individually from polluting the environment and consuming huge amounts of natural resources. The cost is borne by all. In the United States, gasoline is cheap compared with other countries so individuals have little incentive to economise. Although the world's fishing industry could benefit from international regulation, it is not in the interests of individual fishermen so there is no support for the idea and overfishing continues. Approximately 10% of internet users account for about 75% of use of the internet. These "bandwidth hogs" slow down the resource for everyone else. The practice of slicing, dicing and repackaging subprime loans into collaterised debt obligations may have encouraged individual banks to increase their profits by taking bigger risks, knowing that if borrowers defaulted, losses would be shared collectively; and in any case they believed that no big bank would be allowed to fail. Paying Somali pirates may suit individual firms, but it harms the shipping industry as a whole.

The tragedy of the commons can be avoided if individuals and organisations take responsibility for the collective good and are willing to sacrifice immediate personal gain for long-term greater good.

One reason the London Stock Exchange took so long to streamline its antiquated paper-driven system for settling securities was that the various stakeholders could not agree a design for a new system (see Chapter 8). The securities industry could have learned from the successful installation of the TALISMAN computerised settlement system a generation earlier. Before TALISMAN, brokers and jobbers physically delivered orders to one another's offices; then followed the huge and complicated task of matching hundreds of buying and selling transactions. TALISMAN was a major venture for the stock exchange and members were exposed to unlimited liability. A vote of the entire membership was required to authorise funds for development. The project was delayed for months as members argued. It might have collapsed altogether but for a successful appeal by the then chairman, Nicholas Goodison, to the common good:[8]

> One day a bevy of jobbers would come through the door objecting to a particular aspect of Talisman. I would have to say, "Look, that may be your interest, but I ask you in the interests of the total institution, and of the totality of the savings world, not to press that point."

The trouble is that self-interest does not always give way to the common good.

Herding

Warren Buffett has said: "Be fearful when others are greedy, and greedy when others are fearful." It may be good advice, but it goes against the herding instinct. Herding refers to using the behaviour of others as information. Herding may seem purposeful and intelligent, but it is based on false logic. For example, in a street full of restaurants, it may seem wise to choose the busiest one. Surely so many people cannot be wrong. Yet the restaurant may be full only because the first diner made a random choice and others simply followed.

Herding can be a powerful driver. For instance, research into competitive bidding has shown that the more bids there are for an item, the more likely it is that more people will join the auction. Likewise, the herding instinct may tempt well-qualified and experienced investment managers to abandon their own carefully researched stock-picking recommendations and follow the herd. The ultimate form of herding is the speculative bubble (asset prices deviate from intrinsic values), such as the Dutch tulip mania of the 1630s where contracts for bulbs soared to a level ten times higher than the annual income of a skilled craftsman. From February 1998 to February 2000, the internet sector earned returns on equity of over 1,000% – an effect that had disappeared by the end of 2000. Then there was the mid-2000s housing bubble caused by easy credit and low interest rates.

Insanity, said Einstein, is repeating a mistake while expecting better results. Indeed, collapsed bubbles are often followed by echo bubbles. Echo bubbles represent a rekindling of enthusiasm and a repeat of an earlier mistake. We know that echo bubbles happen, but not why. Speculators may simply have short memories. A more plausible possibility is that they cannot believe that their dream-like assumptions of limitless economic growth, be it tulips, internet companies or the property market, were wrong. Herding offers psychological security. That security may prove short-lived. It can also prove costly.

The attraction of herding is psychological safety. Self-confidence is the cure. Emphatically, that does not mean hiring a personal coach or entering into counselling sessions. Rather it means studying a problem thoroughly and drawing your own conclusions. For instance, perhaps because it lost out heavily when the internet bubble burst, Credit Suisse divested itself of risky positions well before the subprime bubble burst. Similarly, some investment managers did their homework properly, and as result steered clients away from Bernard Madoff's superficially attractive but fraudulent funds. Such independence of mind is not psychological. It is primarily analytical and can therefore be practised by anyone.

The missing hero

On March 13th 1964, a young woman named Kitty Genovese was raped and then stabbed to death in New York. Apparently over 30 people watched the attack from their windows, but no one called the police. The incident happened not despite multiple bystanders, but because there were so many bystanders. Everyone assumed (wrongly) that someone else would act. Sometimes referred to as the "Genovese syndrome", the story is frequently cited as a tragic example of people failing to exercise responsibility – hence the allusion to the missing hero.

Firms are vulnerable to the "missing hero" syndrome because formal structures and rules cannot cover everything. Inevitably, there are gaps, power vacuums and decisions that are liable to fall between two stools unless someone takes responsibility, regardless of whether it is their job. In December 2009, heavy snow caused five trains to become stuck in the Channel Tunnel. Travellers, including parents with young families returning from Christmas trips to Euro Disney in Paris, were left stranded for up to 14 hours on failed trains with no food, water, heat or light. Conditions became so bad on one train that passengers resorted to using the end carriage as a lavatory. Eurotunnel, which owns and operates the Channel Tunnel, did little to help the train's operator, Eurostar, which was in charge. But this was an emergency. It did not matter whose job it was to organise a rescue. Yet no one stepped forward to take responsibility.

Public-sector agencies are particularly prone to buck passing. In the UK, Gordon Brown's decision to split financial supervision between three regulatory organisations meant that no one body had overall responsibility for curbing the financial recklessness that led to the global financial crisis.

The answer to the missing hero syndrome is to cultivate a culture where people take responsibility. The word "culture" is important. Clarifying roles, restating who is accountable for what, may help reduce ambiguity, but it can never eradicate it because ambiguity is endemic in organisations. Contrary to what management textbooks may say, responsibility is not something that can be doled out from on high. Responsibility exists only where it is accepted. Otherwise there is no responsibility.

Vicious circle or exploding cluster

A vicious circle exists where decision-makers' efforts to avoid something create the very problem they are trying so hard to avoid.

Then, as they redouble their efforts to avoid the problem, they amplify the destructive spiral. For instance, farmers in Syria have to buy grain to feed their animals because the grass is poor as water is in short supply throughout the Middle East. Since crops have also failed, grain prices have risen. Farmers are therefore forced to sell their sheep and goats to buy grain. Because of the surfeit of sheep and goats coming onto the market, livestock prices have plummeted. Consequently, many herds have shrunk from 50 beasts to five as the agrarian economy collapses.

Some vicious circles resemble exploding clusters. For instance, in order to justify their existence, bureaucrats typically generate work for one another, commissioning audits, seeking information and even auditing audits. The result is an explosion of non-productive work. It is one reason why overheads can spiral.

Deviations have a habit of multiplying into exploding clusters. Just as a faulty component in an aircraft can trigger a chain of increasingly unpredictable reactions that eventually results in catastrophe, one late payer within a supply chain of small and medium-sized firms can create a domino effect that can endanger the whole network. Similarly, the earthquake that struck Japan in March 2011 showed how a shortage of just one critical component could endanger a whole production line.

Self-fulfilling and self-destroying prophecies

A self-fulfilling prophecy creates its own outcome. A forecast of a fuel shortage usually creates one as worried motorists keep topping up their tanks. Similarly, when floods destroyed part of Pakistan's cotton crop in 2010, analysts forecast a shortage. This prompted mills to buy up supplies, creating the very shortage that had been predicted. Hedge funds can create self-fulfilling prophecies. As they start betting against a firm, they may prompt a wave of selling that depresses share prices, so the prediction comes true. If marketing departments believe that a new product has little chance of success, they may invest few resources to promote the product, thus guaranteeing failure. If we believe that our chances of securing a job are slim, we may put little effort into the application form, thus ensuring rejection.

Theories can also become self-fulfilling. More precisely, a theory need not be accurate for it to be popular. All theories are simplified models of the world that stop us from drowning in complexity. To be popular a theory has to be interesting. Interesting theories can become self-fulfilling prophecies because people start acting in a manner that creates the conditions that favour the predictions made in the theory. For example, option pricing, one of the most influential theories in the history of economics, expresses the price of an option as a function of observable parameters and of the hidden volatility of the price of the underlying asset. When the Black-Scholes option pricing theory was first introduced, it was a poor predictor of prices on the Chicago Board Options Exchange. Deviations of 30–40% were common. Yet eventually, deviations were less than 3%. What had changed? It is thought that increased accuracy resulted because people and firms began acting as if the theory were true. For example, market participants began basing their bids on the theoretical value sheets derived from the Black-Scholes model. Moreover, the Autoquote software used the theory to provide traders with theoretical prices for all the options being traded. In short, the theory created the kind of markets it predicted.

Self-destroying prophecies also arise. For example, if big crowds are predicted at sporting events, prospective spectators may decide to stay away. If share issues are expected to be extremely popular, some investors may decide that it is not worth applying as they have little prospect of securing a significant allocation, so the issue is a relative flop. Either form of prophecy creates an outcome that would not otherwise exist.

Paradoxes

Intuitively we might think that "more" of a good thing is better. Although this may be true up to a point, nothing gets better indefinitely. The medieval monasteries became too wealthy for their own good. As rural populations in India become wealthier and demand for meat grows, governments have encouraged smallholders to produce more. Intensified stocking of pigs, chickens and other animals kept in backyards has resulted in poor hygiene. For instance, more than

9% of meat has been found to contain tapeworm cysts. Moreover, high stock densities coupled with close contact with humans have resulted in the emergence of "hot spots", with diseases such as Congo fever, which produces internal bleeding and liver failure with fatal consequences in about 30% of cases.

Firms can also have too much of a good thing. High levels of employee commitment are indeed desirable. Research has consistently shown that employees who are more committed stay longer, are more reliable and practise more organisational citizenship. Yet as some firms have discovered, loyal employees may become time servers who are resistant to change.

The same applies to continuous improvement. Improving existing products and services is usually cheaper and less risky than devising new ones. But the strategy can become self-defeating if obsolete designs are perpetuated. The steam engine could have been made faster and more efficient, but there was no point in channelling resources into research and development once diesel and electric traction arrived. Netbook computers could probably be improved to give longer battery life and so forth, but firms might do better to direct resources into developing tablet computing.

Icarus owned a pair of wax wings that enabled him to fly. But he flew too close to the sun and his wings melted, sending him plunging to his death in the Aegean Sea. In *The Icarus Paradox*, Danny Miller suggests that successful firms can suffer a similar fate.[6] Just as the wings that enabled him to fly became Icarus's downfall, the very strengths that enable a firm to grow may eventually destroy it. For instance, innovative firms can succumb to gratuitous invention. Firms that have succeeded through being cautious may become entrenched and avoid risks that on economic grounds they should take. Icarus died not because he was a high-flyer as such, but because he flew where he shouldn't have.

Anticipate or trip ...

Solutions create new problems, therefore it is wise to try to anticipate how a decision might play out in practice. In particular, how could something "good" become "bad"? Reducing reliance on fossil fuels is "good". Yet more use of biofuels to achieve this objective creates new problems. For instance, it is foreseeable that higher demand for crops will drive up food prices and create pollution – and biofuels may not be particularly efficent either. The question is whether the cure is worse than the disease.

In the West failure is typically seen as "bad" and success as "good". Yet failure may simply mean that the status quo is unchanged whereas, as the medieval monastic foundations discovered, success may contain the ingredients of future calamity. Arthur Andersen, once one of the "big five" seemingly impregnable international accounting firms, with 85,000 employees worldwide, built a strong consultancy practice to complement its traditional auditing business. The consultancy arm became so successful that it eventually accounted for about half of Arthur Andersen's revenue. Yet that success became the firm's undoing. When Enron, an American energy company, failed, the public perception was that Arthur Andersen might have behaved unethically when auditing Enron's accounts because of the conflict of interest created by selling consultancy to Enron. As Enron tottered, Arthur Andersen began shredding documents prompting clients to desert and the firm collapsed. Similarly, the alleged sticky Toyota accelerator pedals were a symptom of a deeper problem, namely the company's expansion ambitions. The resultant dash for growth strained supply lines and led to Toyota using new and inexperienced suppliers in eastern Europe, making supervision difficult. In short, Toyota failed to anticipate what new problems the solution to its current problem might bring.

... and query the control dials

Control systems should alert firms to emerging problems. In practice, they can have the opposite effect by lulling firms into a false sense of security. For example, UBS was one of the most highly regarded banks in the world. With no fewer than 3,000 risk-assessment managers in post, senior management had every reason to believe that the bank was being prudently managed. The chief risk officer was a full member of the group executive board and head of the risk committee. The group chief executive and the vice-president of the board of directors were also members of the risk committee. Even so, UBS lost €50 billion in the American mortgage market and was accused of breaking American law on cross-border transactions. This badly damaged Switzerland's financial industry, not least by weakening Swiss banks' customer secrecy. Following the announcement of write-downs, UBS's reputation changed overnight. It was claimed that the bank had no solid footing and had been run like a hedge fund. In other words, the elaborate systems of control and apparently immaculate corporate governance turned out to be like the fabled emperor's new clothes – there was nothing there.

How can appearances be so deceptive? The mistake was placing too much faith in control systems. Inspections, audits, risk-management systems and all the other trappings of corporate governance are part of the ceremonial. The real purpose is to maintain confidence that everything is as it should be. This is achieved by not looking too hard. For instance, hospitals are assessed on the number of patients treated, not the number cured. Suppliers are rated on whether they have strategies in place to promote equal opportunities, not whether the strategies work. Auditors check whether orders for equipment have been properly raised and matched to invoices, not whether the money has been well spent. Boards of trustees accept reports at face value. Ostensibly, the purpose of so-called stress tests is to root out rogue banks. Their real role is to restore faith in the banking system by providing a symbolic reassurance that something is being done to prevent another global financial crisis. Risk and compliance managers check whether controls are in place, not whether they are relevant. Calamity struck UBS not despite the elaborate system of checks and balances but more likely because of it. Senior management should have recognised that mere compliance does not guarantee safety. It is safest to imagine auditors, risk managers and the like as zombies. They go through the motions. But there is no one there.

If the front door is closed ...

Rather than allowing solutions to define problems, or doing things the way they have always been done, decision-makers should ask: "What is the best way to do this"? This may involve taking an indirect path.

For instance, Audi, BMW and Mercedes are long-standing rivals. But whereas BMW and Mercedes vie with one another to be the biggest volume manufacturers, Audi is aiming to win on quality rather than quantity. Similarly, rather than placing all its hopes on selling more engines in a difficult aviation market, Rolls-Royce also sells maintenance contracts. The strategy is not foolproof because airlines fly fewer miles during economic downturns. Even so, it promises to generate a stream of revenue as engines are routinely returned for servicing year after year. Lesson: if the front door is closed, try the side door.

Paradoxical thinking can stimulate innovation and creativity. For example, the idea that less can be more is reflected in the design of the Mazda MX5 sports car. It stresses simplicity. Simple designs are cheap to produce and are often more robust in service. This makes the car cheap to buy and cheap to run. Porsche managed a similar feat with the Boxster Spyder. The car is basically a lighter and therefore faster version of the Boxster S – minus the electric hood. It is also more expensive. Usually the approach to creating more expensive cars is to add features. The MX5 and the Boxster Spyder show what subtraction can achieve.

Wachtell, Lipton, Rosen & Katz became one of America's most highly regarded firms by taking the indirect path. The foundations of its success were laid in 1965 when the founding partners decided that above all they wanted interesting careers. They resolved not to become a full service firm because that meant undertaking routine work. Instead, they specialised in partners' areas of interest and eventually became best known as adviser of last resort for firms facing hostile takeovers. Moreover, unlike conventional law firms, Wachtell decided against forming long-term relationships with clients, restricting itself to transaction-based relationships. Another break with custom was employing comparatively few associates. Conventional law firms make most of their money by extracting a surplus from salaried associates who receive only a fraction of the revenues they generate and usually have little hope of becoming partners. Wachtell's philosophy was to employ associates only if they displayed partnership potential. Moreover, the emphasis was distinctly collegiate, with everyone expected to draft briefs and do research.

A further break with tradition was charging according to the value of the work to the client, rather than the industry practice of hourly rates. Although that made Wachtell expensive to employ, this was counterbalanced by the firm's intense commitment to serving clients. Wachtell prides itself on treating everything as a crisis, worrying so that the client does not have to. Clients also know that their affairs receive partners' attention and that quality is paramount, as lawyers will work 20 hours to improve a document by 2%. "They're expensive because they don't use so many people," said a client. "Why do you pay a little bit more? Well, the quality of the work. The timeliness."[7] Just as the medieval monasteries became wealthy by accident, Wachtell's exceptional success came because it put job satisfaction before money.

Loose-tight virtues

Often our unbridled efforts to avoid something can create the very situation we tried hard to avoid. For example, car sellers, anxious not to lose touch with prospective customers, invest in elaborate computer systems and instruct sales staff to record names, addresses and other details before discussing the customer's requirements. But customers may resent the interrogation and refuse to co-operate. So the solution creates the very problem that sellers are striving to avoid. A better idea would be to allow sales staff to judge when it is appropriate to take details and to use their discretion about the method used. It may be better to record details on paper and enter them into the computer after the customer has left the showroom. This may be less efficient than direct entry, but some customers find computers intrusive.

Such situations may be avoided by adopting "loose-tight" control, which recognises that trying to control everything is a mistake. It is better to allow employees autonomy over most things while maintaining tight control over a few important things. "Loose-tight" usually means more control, not less. Similarly, rather than create chaos by trying to impose order, it may be better to acknowledge organised chaos – that is, to look for the order that may exist in what appears to be chaos – to recognise that contradictions can coexist in, for example, notions of "flexible-specialisation" and "dynamic-stability". Part of the art of management is making these tensions productive.

Virtuous circles can be triggered by paradoxical thinking. The philosophy of total quality management works on the principle of investing to improve work processes, reduce complaints, scrap and rework so production becomes cheaper. Since the finished product is better and therefore more attractive to customers, the firm becomes more profitable. Whereas vicious circles result from repeating ineffective actions, a virtuous circle is one where beneficial actions automatically reproduce themselves.

Dare to act counter-intuitively

Intuitive reactions to problems are often wrong. For example, when a strategy fails, the intuitive approach is to apply more of the same – usually only making things worse. When the factory system gained momentum, the guilds reacted by trying to impose more control. This merely strengthened the incentive to circumnavigate the guilds. Similarly, McDonald's thrived on the "eat up and ship out" principle by designing outlets to discourage lingering – with hard seats, for example. Intuitively, the global economic crisis called for more of the same – that is, even harder seats to increase turnover by getting customers to eat up and ship out even faster. Instead, McDonald's abandoned the trusty formula and reinvested in its outlets, refurnishing and redecorating restaurants to make them pleasant places to sit in. This counter-intuitive strategy worked. Similarly, Walmart avoided the temptation to create more of the same by opening more big stores. Instead, the company recognised that it could achieve its growth ambitions by opening lots of small convenience stores. In business, as in war, the indirect approach often works best.

The reason firms are reluctant to try counter-intuitive approaches is because at first sight they seem silly, or even suicidal. For instance, the late W. Edwards Deming, a pioneer of total quality management, urged firms to ignore the competition and instead focus upon meeting the customer's needs. This may seem suicidal yet it is actually very wise. For instance, the Marriott hotel chain applied this philosophy by designing rooms to meet guests' needs, supplying comfortable beds, duvets and reading lamps with the mantra "above and beyond". By ignoring competition benchmarks, the Marriott chain set new industry standards. Those innovations may have made only marginal improvements but marginal advantages can be important. Who dares wins.

Leaving the party

Nothing gets better and better indefinitely. The question is when to stop. Brand exploitation is an example. How many more items should firms like Dunhill add to their prodigious list? Mont Blanc may be on terra firma selling watches and luxury leather goods as well as pens, but is shower gel going too far? Is it worth trying to fly just a little higher by adding one more product, taking one more risk, and pushing the brand just a little bit further?

The lesson is to quit while you are ahead. It is the difference between maximising and optimising. Maximising involves extracting the last drop of advantage from a situation. It is like getting the last piece of coal out of a drift mine that is becoming increasingly expensive to work. In contrast, optimising means recognising that you have probably had the best of something and moving on. In other words, don't push your luck.

Symbolic importance

"Executives", said Tom Peters, "don't synthesise chemicals or operate lift trucks ... they deal in symbols."[9] Indeed, symbols can be more important than substance. According to the textbooks, functions like strategic planning, customer care and risk assessment are essential elements of rational management. It is unwise to place too much faith in them, however, as their main role may be to make it look as if a firm is being managed responsibly. For example, customers who complain when their toasters break or hotel guests who complain about slow room service may receive a letter of apology, free samples or vouchers. Such gestures provide reassurance that a company cares about the quality of its products or services, not that it will re-engineer its systems to make sure it never happens again. Grievance procedures exist not to resolve problems, but to manage conflict by deflecting it into official channels. Consultation and negotiation mechanisms make it look as if firms are empowering employees and stakeholders. Non-executive directors are appointed to suggest that outside expertise and experience are valued.

In 2009 Huawei Technologies, a global telecommunications supply business, was named second-largest maker of mobile-network equipment after Ericsson, following expansion in Europe and developing countries. Major American contracts, however, have eluded the company, ostensibly because of concerns about security. In 2008, the American government blocked Huawei's acquisition of 3Com, an American network-equipment manufacturer, because 3Com supplies the Pentagon with equipment to protect it from cyber-attacks. Huawei has since offered to establish an advisory committee, to allow access to source codes, and to allow security experts to check its products to verify that they do not contain technology that would enable spying or render computer networks liable to attack. The experts include an American company, Electronic Warfare Associates. Customers would also be able to choose whether or not to use Huawei engineers for servicing.

Huawei's careful attention to symbols may help to open doors in the American market. Cultivating the various authorities may help to break down resistance because it suggests that the company takes its responsibilities seriously and respects expertise. Simply establishing an advisory committee builds trust, regardless of what the committee actually does. It is the difference between doing things right and doing the right things. Above all, what matters is being seen to do the right things.

Similarly, research has shown that nascent entrepreneurs are more likely to attract loans if they seem to be already successful. For example, the simple mention of an MBA qualification from a prestigious business school or the distribution of small well-made gifts bearing the company logo can inspire confidence. The owner of a threadbare start-up said:[10]

> I think cash is absolutely king and you have to be very, very parsimonious with your cash. If you can get a discount, like second-hand computers – why do you want new computers? You don't. I've

got second-hand computers. Okay, fine. Have a small office. What matters is the external presentation, your perceived office.

Another winning way is drawing attention to achievements and awards (even if products or services have not yet been marketed). So is trading on the names of prestigious associates and using exceptionally rigorous recruitment techniques to impress potential employees. Going to the trouble of producing a glossy brochure can lead people to infer that a start-up firm must be fairly good if it can find the money for advertising. Quibbling over contractual terms also creates a good impression, as it makes it look as if the firm is not desperate for money.

Similarly, what is needed to persuade prospective investors who might otherwise run a mile is a respectable board of directors on the headed notepaper, a pledge to follow corporate governance codes and a listing on the London Stock Exchange, preferably the FTSE index.

Economists say that survival depends upon efficiency – converting inputs into outputs using the fewest resources. This is entirely rational. And wrong. Social acceptance matters more.

Firms that break socially prescribed boundaries will be denied resources and/or experience extreme environmental turbulence. For instance, when allegations of phone hacking gained momentum, the *News of the World* suddenly found firms such as Ford cancelling advertising space. Similarly, Nike, an American sportswear company, has pledged to improve its sourcing after reports of abuse of workers' rights in factories in places like Indonesia and Taiwan. Pharmaceutical companies that deny drugs to HIV sufferers in poor countries risk governments refusing to honour their patents. Revelations about his private life almost destroyed Tiger Woods's brand image. Swiss banks are being forced to swap their tradition of secrecy for a more socially acceptable cult of privacy by agreeing to tax customers' accounts and to remit the proceeds to governments. The alternative is for governments to make it impossible for citizens to set up Swiss bank accounts. The United States did precisely that after a dispute with UBS about Americans using the bank to evade domestic taxes. Just as we only discover a firm's culture when we go against it, we only know for sure where the informal boundaries lie when we cross them. By then it is too late. The damage is done. As Warren Buffett said, it can take 20 years to build a reputation and five minutes to lose it. If public sensitivities are involved, the best policy is safety first.

When being wrong is right

Decisions are more likely to be viewed favourably if supported by a battery of expert thinking and advice. Firms appoint prestigious firms of lawyers, accountants, investment managers, and so forth, because having household names on the headed notepaper enhances credibility. Moreover, if a household name pronounces a course of action to be sound, decision-makers are entitled to believe it. If the advice should prove to be wrong (Enron, Barings and UBS were all audited by household names), decision-makers are protected from blame. In other words, it is often better for decision-makers to be wrong for the right reasons than to go it alone. Going it alone risks being seen as acting irresponsibly.

When evaluating ideas, decision-makers should guard against being overly influenced by prestige. For instance, Netscape Communications used its authority to influence internet-browser standards. Such was the credibility of the leadership team that other people in the industry believed that if the team thought this was the way to go, they must be right.

Must be right? Household names are relied on not because they are right, but because they are household names – and because they have been right in the past or are perceived to offer an acceptable standard. Scientists who work for established firms such as HP and IBM are more likely to be listened to than those who work for start-up companies. But that does not make them right. A textbook becomes an authority not because it is right, but because people consult it regularly. Similarly, industry leaders may support an idea, but there may be better ideas struggling to gain acceptance. What matters is the quality of the idea, not the source.

8 The march of folly: the escalation trap

"If at first you don't succeed, try, try again. Then quit. No use being a damn fool about it."

W.C. Fields

IN 1961 SOMETHING REMARKABLE HAPPENED in the Libyan desert. Eight years earlier in 1953 an American entrepreneur named Bunker Hunt applied for a drilling licence. The prospects were exciting as geologists advised Hunt that an oilfield recently discovered in Algeria would almost certainly extend into Libya. Unfortunately for Hunt, the so-called "Seven Sisters" (multinational oil companies) were already drilling in the best sites. The only concession available was so far from the Algerian border and offered such miserable prospects that even the customary bribe to local officials was waived:[1]

> The story could have ended there ... except for Bunker's instinct. As a gambling man, he believed that the more cards he could draw on, the better his chances would be, even if the cards were those no one else thought worth picking up.

Indeed, Hunt drilled for years and found nothing. Moreover, despite their markedly better chances, the "Seven Sisters" did no better drilling near Algeria. Eventually, one of them – British Petroleum (BP) – went into partnership with Hunt. The teams struck out into the desert and started drilling. One well after another was reported dry. The rig superintendent was instructed by BP to stop drilling and return home. It was the final shattering blow for Hunt, who had invested all his money in the venture:[2]

Then, just for luck, the rig superintendent drilled another ten feet into the sand before withdrawing the bit from the third hole, and, in doing so, uncovered Bunker's ace. That ten feet was enough to pierce the cap of one of the world's largest oil fields.

What if the decision to drill down another 10 feet had proved abortive? Would the rig superintendent have been tempted to drill down another 10 feet, and then another? If at first you don't succeed, says the proverb, try, try, try again. To a point the maxim is sound. Few complex projects go smoothly. If decision-makers gave up at the first sign of trouble, little would be accomplished. Yet there are limits. Taken too far, persistence can be self-defeating. In January 2004 Deloitte & Touche, the liquidators of BCCI (Bank of Credit and Commerce International), began suing the Bank of England for £850m over its supervision of BCCI's collapse in 1991. Although it was apparent to legal experts from day one that the case was hopeless – the Bank of England acknowledged that supervision was inadequate but denied acting dishonestly – Deloitte persisted for almost two years before finally accepting that persistence was no longer in the best interests of creditors, leaving a £100m legal bill. Big oil companies have been drilling Kazakhstan's Kashagan oilfield for ten years. So far they have nothing to show for $20 billion of investment. Even if oil is discovered, the field is difficult, dangerous and would cost an estimated $137 billion to develop. Proton, a Malaysian car company, acquired Lotus in 1996. In the next 16 years, Lotus made a profit only once. Why persist?

We know a lot more about how to get organisations moving than how to stop them when they begin moving in the wrong direction. Changing direction may sometimes be necessary to redirect resources to more profitable projects. In theory, redirection is straightforward. Economics offers clear and simple guidance: that is, when a project looks as if it might fail, decision-makers should reassess it. Having reassessed it, they should reinvest only if future benefits are likely to exceed future costs. In practice, decision-makers may be tempted to persist with poor projects well beyond an economically defensible point only to end up "throwing good money after bad" – a phenomenon known as escalation of commitment. Why should decision-makers sometimes behave so foolishly? This chapter explores what drives escalation and how decision-makers can avoid becoming embroiled in a spiral of escalating commitment.

Too much promise

Escalation often starts with bright promises. Project planners are as prone to overconfidence as anyone else (see Chapter 1). For instance, United Artists was ecstatic when Michael Cimino agreed to produce the film *Heaven's Gate*. Cimino's previous film, *The Deer Hunter*, had been a huge box-office success and *Heaven's Gate* promised to repeat history. Certain that it could not fail with Cimino in charge, United Artists agreed to all his conditions, including complete artistic freedom and complete control over the making of the film. Cimino held United Artists to the contract. He locked the film away while it was being made, so it was only when the project was hugely overspent and well behind schedule that United Artists began to realise the enormity of its mistake. *Heaven's Gate* was dire – though it has since attained cult status. United Artists spent $42m making the film. Box-office receipts were just $3m. Had United Artists not been so confident about appointing Cimino and insisted upon having oversight of the project, it could have intervened sooner and saved itself a lot of money.

Similarly, the seeds of failure are often sown early on as project planners promise more than they can realistically hope to deliver. They do this because they know resources are scarce and in choosing which projects to pursue, firms look at which will deliver the most desirable outcomes. Thus there is a temptation to gild the lily. Estimated costs and timescales are pared down and projected revenues and other benefits scaled up to make the venture look as attractive as possible. For example, research has shown that in big projects cost overruns and benefit shortfalls of 50% happen regularly. Moreover, cost overruns of 100% are by no means unknown. Sydney Opera House in Australia holds the world record for over-optimism. The estimated cost was A$7m. Construction started in 1959. The building opened in 1973, ten years late, at a cost of A$102m – an overrun of 1,400% – and this was for a scaled-down version of the original design. The estimated cost of the refurbishment of London's

Savoy Hotel was £120m. Work began in late 2007. The timescale was 18 months. In the end, the project took nearly three years to complete and cost £200m.

Another problem is that planners sometimes use irrelevant "anchors" (see Chapter 2) to formulate estimates. Moreover, even if planners recognise that the anchor is either too high or too low, they seldom adjust their estimates adequately. An example is the building of the Channel Tunnel between England and France. Prospective investors were promised that construction would be fairly straightforward. A 10% allowance for contingencies was therefore deemed sufficient. Even if the venture cost a little more, investors were assured the revenues would more than compensate. There would be plenty to go round. The final cost was almost double the original estimate, however, and revenues turned out to be less than a third of what investors were promised. The plans proved to be hopelessly wrong because the anchors used to estimate costs, revenues and timescales were derived from projects that involved tunnelling through mountains and under rivers. These anchors were inappropriate for such a challenging venture.

You are invited to bid for $1. There is no reserve price so the prize could be yours for as little as 1 cent. But there is one condition: this is a special kind of auction where the second highest bidder must pay the bid price but receives nothing. Would you bid?

In classroom auctions students typically bid for fun. Mischievously they drive up the price and then drop out, leaving two of their fellows trapped. The auction serves to show how competition can fuel escalation. No one wins because bidding invariably rises well above the face value of the prize. It is a metaphor for the potentially suicidal price wars waged between airlines, supermarkets and newspapers. (There is another version of the auction whereby all bidders must pay but only the highest bidder receives the coin.) The main learning point is that although bidders may enter the auction for fun planning to drop out, it is risky. No one intends to become trapped but inevitably this is precisely what happens to two bidders. The lesson is to stay out altogether.

Games people play

Firms bidding for contracts may be tempted to submit artificially low bids to win the tender if they are reasonably sure that delays and cost overruns will be tolerated, as they often are by public-sector organisations. Similarly, public servants may underestimate costs, sometimes to ensure that a project gets approval and sometimes to please their political masters. For instance, the provincial government insisted that spending on the 2010 Vancouver Olympic Games would not exceed C$765m. Yet in 2006 when plans were still embryonic, British Columbia's auditor-general calculated that with essential infrastructure projects such as a new rail link to the airport, the games would actually cost provincial taxpayers C$2.5 billion. Even so, the games went ahead. There is a lot of job rotation in the public sector. Consequently, those who compile the unrealistic estimates know that by the time the real costs materialise, they will have moved on and the government will simply have to find the extra money.

Escalating IT

IT projects are particularly prone to escalation. An example is the TAURUS project. After the October 1987 crash, banks and securities firms discovered that the system for settling securities contracts was in chaos. Locked into the confusion were almost 1m outstanding transactions, worth about £13.4 billion at the time. The immediate cause of the problem was the accumulation of privatisation issues. Millions of people had entered the stockmarket, typically dealing in small packets of shares. The underlying problem was the City of London's antiquated paper-driven system for settling securities, which had hardly changed in 200 years since the days when securities transactions were sealed over a glass of sherry and the toast, "who pays". It could take up to three weeks for money and share certificates to change hands. Moreover, it was obvious that the system could not cope with an upsurge in business. Something had to be done. That something was to build TAURUS, an IT-based platform to enable paperless settlement.

Although it was generally agreed that the project was urgent, the City spent two years arguing over the design. The trouble was that all the various stakeholders, banks, custodians, registrars, retail brokers, institutional brokers and so forth had different ideas. The discussions became so complicated that committee meetings were dubbed "the Mad Hatter's tea party". Since no one would give way, the LSE tried to please everyone. As a result the design for TAURUS became extremely complicated. To make matters worse, the City insisted on a maximum timescale of 18 months. Almost everyone connected with the project believed that TAURUS would take longer. A member of the Citywide group set up to monitor the project said:[3]

> I drew some graphs early on, plotting planned deliverables against actual. At one point the graphs weren't even converging. They were showing delivery at infinity. Even when they started to converge they were showing delivery in 1995.

Those graphs would prove to be uncannily accurate. But in 1990, no one took them seriously. The ruling myth was that the timescale was ambitious but achievable. The prospectus promised that TAURUS would cost the London Stock Exchange £50m. Construction began in early 1990. Three years later, in March 1993, the project was cancelled. The LSE had spent over £80m and the City of London an estimated £400m. All that money was lost. Nothing was salvaged from TAURUS.

Francis Bacon said that it is better to begin with doubts and end in certainties. A hallmark of projects like the Sydney Opera House, the Channel Tunnel and TAURUS is that they began with certainty.

A life of their own

Once these poorly appraised projects are approved, they soon gather momentum. For instance, when the London 2012 Olympics were planned, Tessa Jowell, the Olympics minister at the time, insisted that the "absolute limit" on public expenditure was £9.5 billion. By November 2009, that sum had already been exceeded by almost a third. Similarly, when Vancouver's city government planned the 2010 Winter Olympics, they were determined to avoid the losses incurred by other high-profile events. Yet for all the government's resolve, the Olympic village built on the city's waterfront added an unexpected C$458m to the final bill. Costs mount because myriad actors make myriad decisions on their own initiative. Each decision may mean only a small additional cost. But these costs mount up as projects take on a life of their own.

Once a project gets under way, earlier decisions may return to haunt those who made them. The LSE decided that the only hope of meeting the ambitious timescale was to buy a software package named Vista to drive TAURUS rather than build a customised one. Vista is good but it was designed for banking applications, not for the complex UK securities industry. A member of the project team said:[4]

> *So, what's the faster way of building it? You go off and you get a package. I thought, "Oh yes, I don't believe that there are such things upon the shelf to do the sort of things we do." You've got to stop and ask yourself "Why" .... It's a very complex interrelationship, and those, when you model them ... are where the difficulties lie.*

Again, the insight proved prescient. The budget for re-engineering Vista was £4m out of the expected total cost of £50m for the whole project. By the time TAURUS was cancelled, the LSE had spent £14m and the task was nowhere near complete. It shows how one ill-judged decision made early on can have unintended and unwanted repercussions.

In theory, a project fails when it becomes clear that expectations are unlikely to be met. Since in practice few ventures go suddenly and completely awry, decision-makers may be slow to recognise failure. For instance, in 2003, Steiff, makers of luxury teddy bears, shifted about a fifth of its production from Germany to China, aiming to reduce costs. Slowly, the decision turned sour. Steiff discovered that Chinese seamstresses, more accustomed to making computer chips, needed about a year to become fully proficient. Moreover, shipping the bears proved problematic as containers were often booked. Sometimes Steiff would pay money to reserve space then find that the bears were not ready to be shipped. Steiff's strategy of selling low-cost bears also failed. After five years Steiff declared the situation intolerable and reversed the decision. With perfect hindsight, Steiff might have acted sooner. But that was one luxury it did not have.

Denial and delusion

Then there is the quality of feedback. Early on, it is likely to be patchy and unreliable. Even when feedback becomes more consistently negative, it may be wise to persist for a while in order to give a venture every chance of success.

A bigger problem is denial. As best-laid plans go awry, decision-makers may convince themselves that the problems are temporary and/or exaggerated. For instance, pharmaceutical companies may refuse to accept potentially disturbing results from clinical trials arguing that the tests are biased, that the scientists conducting them are incompetent or that their interpretations of the results are too cautious – anything to avoid accepting the inconvenient truth.

Denial is a powerful force. For instance, the original plans for Denver International Airport did not include a fully automated baggage system. As construction commenced, the decision-makers changed their minds. Specifications for an automated system were issued. But of the 16 domestic and foreign firms contacted, only three responded. Worse still, a consulting firm recommended against all three designs because they would not meet the airport's needs and, in any case, could not be built in time for the planned opening. Moreover, one of the firms that elected not to bid was BAE Automated Systems, even though its Telecar system of laser barcode readers and conveyor belts was working successfully in other airports. But the Denver project was much bigger and much more complex than anything BAE had built before. Denver's decision-makers also sought advice from industry experts – with negative results. Yet despite such potentially ominous responses, Denver officials decided to proceed. The project was an expensive failure.

Similarly, drilling for Amsterdam's new underground metro started in 2002. Since then, the cost of the project has almost doubled. Moreover, much of Amsterdam is propped up on wooden stilts. In summer 2008, several buildings along the route suddenly sank a few centimetres. People were forced to escape through their windows. Work on the project was halted temporarily. Yet city leaders refused to believe that this might be an ominous development. This was despite the ombudsman saying that the construction was substandard. When the Apple iPhone4 was released, there were thousands of complaints from users who found that it kept cutting out. At first, Apple refused to believe that the phone was faulty. It accused users of not holding it properly. It was several weeks before Apple acknowledged the problem and fixed it.

Denial protects us from ego-damage. Ego-defensiveness is a powerful escalation driver. This is because it creates blind spots. For instance, research has shown that managers often overrate the performance of staff they have personally appointed. It is as if managers say to themselves, "I appointed them, so they must be good." Those managers may be last to notice deficiencies in those employees.

A symptom of denial is that decision-makers seize upon information that supports their preconceived ideas while downplaying or even ignoring contradictory data. Since this tends to happen unconsciously, decision-makers may genuinely believe that the person they appointed is performing well, that success is close or that they are behaving in an ethically defensible manner – when the opposite is true. For instance, Arthur Andersen's employees may have unconsciously paid undue attention to data that enabled them to justify maintaining the relationship with Enron – a valuable client.

Escalation of commitment

Eventually, failure may become so obvious that denial is useless. Yet this does not mean that firms automatically exit. There may be penalty payments to contractors, leasehold obligations, surplus stock to dispose of, redundancy costs and the costs of dismantling partially completed works to consider. When exit costs are taken into account, it may be nearly as expensive to quit as it is to continue.

The pressures for persistence are likely to be most intense where so-called "long-haul" projects are concerned. That is, major projects requiring a huge financial outlay where there are no revenues to offset costs until the project is finished. Time equals risk. As we plan, the world is changing. Concorde was probably never viable. To make matters worse, it was planned when aviation fuel was cheap. By the time the plane entered service that important assumption no longer applied. It happens: by the time some decisions are implemented the business case for them no longer exists. Likewise, London was committed to hosting the 2012 Olympics long before the global financial crisis started in 2008. By 2009, there were already over 7,500 people working on the London Olympic site. Over 1,000 contracts worth £5 billion had already been signed. Even if it were politically possible to cancel the games, what compensation would the contractors be entitled to? How much more expensive does cancellation become as a project grows to include 100,000–150,000 contractors for catering, cleaning and security work? Similarly, of the 1,100 "Olympic" flats in Vancouver offered to the general public, only a third had been sold by September 2009. Moreover, the global financial crisis resulted in sponsors pulling out. Yet there was no question of cancelling the Winter Olympics because of all the other commitments that had been made. As the saying goes in the aviation industry: take-off is optional, landing is compulsory.

Closing down a major project involves a lot of work and expense. In the North Sea there are about 50,000 oil wells, as well as surface and sub-sea installations and about 10,000km of pipelines. Decommissioning these is likely to cost about £31m. Exiting from a major project can also involve considerable operational disruption, to say nothing of working through all the rules and consultation procedures to deal with the transfer of staff and redundancies. Add to that the renegotiation of contracts. Then there is the political fallout of admitting failure to deal with. Often it is easier not to rock the boat.

Fear of failure – and combatting it

Fear of failure fuels escalation. In an experiment by Barry Staw, a professor at Haas School of Business at the University of California Berkeley, and one of the leading contributors to escalation research, two groups of students study a scenario describing a company that has been in decline for a decade owing to ill-judged R&D decisions. Group 1 was given $10m to invest in R&D and asked to decide which of the two major divisions to support: consumer or industrial products. Participants were asked to justify their decision in writing. They then received feedback. They learnt that, five years later, the company believed an even greater investment in R&D was required and therefore $20m was now available. This time, instead of making an "either/or" decision, participants could divide the money between the two divisions as they saw fit. Again written justification was required. When the results were fed back, half of group 1 learnt that the divisions are now profitable, and the other half learnt that profits had fallen and their decision had failed.

In contrast, group 2 took part only in the second allocation decision. Participants did not decide which division to support initially, but were told that someone else had made the decision. Both groups – those "responsible" for previous decisions and those in the "not responsible" category – again decided how much money to allocate. The result was that participants responsible for an initially unsuccessful decision tended to direct more money to support ailing divisions than those who merely inherited the problem. We can infer from the experiment that those who initiate dud projects may reinvest in them as a way of signalling self-belief in the project and to stave off the impression of failure.

Since fear of failure drives escalation, the more that firms can do to alleviate it the better. Firms should recognise that some projects will fail. Moreover, failure often happens for reasons that are beyond decision-makers' control. Firms should consider rewarding process rather than outcomes. Rewarding process means judging decision-makers on whether they have asked the right questions, made sure the answers are adequate, conducted rigorous analysis of the options and so forth. Rewarding process is controversial. For example, a manager said, "You get lots of process, but very little traction." Ultimately, decision-makers must choose which set of problems they prefer to manage, that is, those produced by pressure for results or those produced by rewarding decision-makers for doing things right regardless of outcomes.

Another option may be to separate the responsibility for conceiving and designing a project from the management of a project. The rationale for bifurcation is to prevent managers from becoming so committed to a venture that they can no longer exercise objective judgment. The downside is that managers who initiate projects may feel demotivated because they never get to see them through. Bifurcation can also encourage an "over the wall" mentality. That is, those who design and initiate projects may not care too much about the practicalities. Delivery is seen as someone else's problem.

Waste not want not

In your fridge you have two takeaway meals. Both have reached their use-by date. The meals are identical except that one cost $12 and the other was bought on special offer for $7. You have to choose which meal to eat. You may opt for the more expensive meal because the decision seems less wasteful. Research has consistently shown that people dislike wasting things or even appearing to be wasteful. Waste includes:

- using resources carelessly;
- using less that you have paid for;
- paying too much for something.

Avoiding waste may be a good thing: "waste not, want not", counsels the proverb. Yet our innate aversion to waste can result in economically poor decisions and fuel escalation.

To be more precise, when benefits are weighed against costs, some forms of waste make sense. In manufacturing, routinely replacing light bulbs, belts and other components suffering wear and tear means components are not fully utilised. Yet that waste is cheaper than dealing with the disruption and loss of production resulting from an item failing in service. Even waste on a grand scale may be justified. When the London Stock Exchange decided to switch to electronic trading in preparation for deregulation (Big Bang) in 1986, many members opposed the plan because it meant closing the trading floor where brokers and jobbers met to conduct business. After failing to persuade members that they would no longer need to leave their offices to conduct business, the LSE gave in and spent £6m on a new trading floor. After barely six weeks members discovered the benefits of screen-based trading. The floor was eventually closed with hardly a murmur of protest. On one level the decision to build it was a complete waste of money. Yet it was probably wise because hostility to screen-based trading subsided. The LSE thus avoided resistance that could have seriously undermined preparations for deregulation. Moral: go with the flow.

The trouble is that decision-makers may ignore costs/benefits logic if it means incurring waste. For instance, experiments have shown that two options may be of equal benefit, but if one seems wasteful it will probably be rejected. This is why mobile-phone companies sometimes offer trade-ins on old handsets rather than offer discounts of an equal amount. In an industry faced with rapid obsolescence, companies try to persuade consumers to change handsets more frequently than necessary. Likewise, in an effort to stimulate the car industry following the global financial crisis in 2008, the governments of France and Germany offered money to motorists to trade in their old (at least nine or ten years) cars for new or nearly new. Again, the aim of the scheme was to make the decision seem less wasteful.

In theory, sophisticated firms should not have this problem. They employ accountants to calculate costs and benefits and advise decision-makers accordingly. Even so, when choosing between maximising utility and incurring waste, it may well be utility that is sacrificed. For instance, research has shown that individuals are more likely to abandon a failing project if they can sell it for $500,000 to someone who will use it, than if the only option is to sell it for scrap for $500,000.

Sunk costs

Sunk costs can also make quitting hard. Sunk costs refer to investments made in anticipation of benefits. They should normally be ignored when deciding how to allocate resources. This is because the existence of sunk costs cannot change outcomes. For example, if an oilfield is barren, it makes no sense to keep drilling – no matter how much the drilling licence cost. Even so, sunk costs are not always sunk psychologically. Research has shown that the more we pay for an item the more likely we are to use it.[5] The correct approach is to base decisions on future costs and benefits, not sunk costs.

Yet future benefits are not always considered properly. Research has shown that firms are more likely to invest $1m to finish a project if they have already invested $10m than if they have invested nothing. Moreover, that applies even though they have no information about future returns.

Time, effort and emotional energy also count as sunk costs. A study of bidding on eBay found that sellers who dispensed with reserve prices and started with very low bids tended to achieve higher prices than sellers who imposed a reserve price. We can infer from this that starting low without a reserve price encourages bidding. As the price rises, early bidders must invest additional time and effort if they wish to remain in the auction. Eventually, early bidders may be so reluctant to forgo their investment that they become determined to acquire the item at all costs. Likewise, research has shown that entrepreneurs are more likely to sell businesses they have bought than businesses they put a lot of time into establishing themselves and to which they they have a strong emotional attachment, even though their own start-ups are making less money than bought businesses.

A question of framing

Are you a risk seeker? Which would you prefer:

- To incur a definite loss of $50,000, or a 50% chance of losing $100,000?
- To incur a definite loss of $50,000, or a 50% chance of losing $500,000?

Another escalation driver concerns how problems are expressed (framed). For example, when decisions are framed negatively, decision-makers see themselves as having to choose between losses. That is, they must choose between a definite loss (like $50,000) and the chance to avoid that loss altogether, but at the risk of incurring a worse loss. Research has shown that when problems are expressed negatively, decision-makers tend to become risk seeking. That is, they prefer the second of the two options.[6]

To be risk seeking is to take a bigger risk than the odds warrant. Shell made this mistake. In 2004 the company was fined £17m by the Financial Services Authority for mis-stating reserves. Why did it do this? Shell may have decided that straightforward disclosure would harm the share price. That is, it would mean a definite loss. Tinkering with the formula for calculating reserves offered the chance of avoiding that loss, but at the risk of subsequently incurring a much bigger one if the ploy was discovered – as indeed it was. Similarly, decisions concerning faltering projects are often expressed as a choice between losses. Risk-seeking behaviour may explain (but not excuse) why so many airport developments experience severe teething problems. For instance, the opening of Heathrow's £4.36 billion Terminal 5 dissolved into chaos. Hong Kong's Chek Lap Kok airport experienced computer problems that delayed flights and baggage-handling systems. Moreover, these problems persisted for months and did huge reputational damage. Denver, Bangkok and Kuala Lumpur all had similar experiences. Rather than incur the ignominy of opening late – a definite loss – airport authorities prefer to risk a much bigger loss by pressing ahead and opening the airport without thoroughly testing new systems and novel technology. Hard though it may be, sometimes it is better to brave a definite loss than risk the alternative. Besides, risk-seeking behaviour happens because of the way the problem is expressed (framed), that is, as a choice between losses. Decision-makers can escape this psychological trap simply by reframing the problem.

Public image

Admitting failure privately is hard enough. Admitting it publicly is likely to be even harder. No one wants to look foolish. Moreover, in Western society leaders are expected to appear resolute and decisive. Those who take their time before making important decisions risk being seen as weak and vacillating. Western society also values consistency. We are expected to keep our promises, to stick to our decisions, to finish what we have started and generally be "not for turning" no matter what happens. For instance, in an experiment, two groups of participants were invited to set limits on their involvement in an investment decision before committing funds and before receiving feedback. One group was required to set limits in public; the other was allowed to do this in private. Those who set limits in public typically stopped investing when the limits were reached even though the economic data said continue. Asked why they behaved in such an economically irrational manner, participants said they thought it would "look good" to be seen to carry out their publicly avowed intentions.

Preventing escalation

Bad projects take resources from good ones. When the Channel Tunnel was completed, Alistair Morton, then chairman of Eurotunnel, allegedly said that if the true cost had been known at the outset, the project would never have been started. Indeed, what might we have had instead? As stated earlier, large IT projects are particularly prone to escalation. Researchers at Oxford University studied almost 1,500 IT projects in the UK. One in six went over budget by more than 200%. A similar pattern of failure was also found in Europe and the United States. Invisibility is one problem. Unlike building a bridge, there is little to see. Consequently, IT projects are hard to monitor. Another problem concerns the language barrier that may exist between engineers and decision-makers. Requirements are often poorly understood to begin with. Moreover, things get lost in translation into software codes. These problems can be so tortuous that the researchers recommend that firms should commission such projects only if they can withstand a 400% cost overrun. Another pertinent question is the opportunity cost.

Since most projects become progressively harder to stop once they get under way, a gram of prevention is worth a kilo of cure. As noted earlier, failure is often traceable to poor planning. No plan survives contact with reality. Yet although the results are always different from the plan, they are usually better than if there is no plan at all. This is because the planning process forces decision-makers to experience the future and organise accordingly.

Yet it is equally important to recognise why the results never match the plan. Planning is symbolically important because it imparts an air of control over uncertainty (see Chapter 4). Planning also makes risky decisions appear rational. For example, when the Canadian government agreed to host the "Expo 86" trade fair, it insisted that it should at least break even. To meet that requirement, planners assumed that every man, woman and child in Canada would visit the fair at least once. They did not. Similarly, although the projected attendance figures for the Commonwealth Games in New Delhi looked impressive, attendance was well below what was forecast. Decision-makers should remind themselves that even the best plans are only educated guesses. They can never be anything more because the assumptions on which the plans are based cannot be verified.

Because planners sometimes use inappropriate anchors, the "figures behind the figures" should always be probed. For example:

- Where do the estimates come from?
- How relevant are they to the current project?
- What adjustments have been made?
- How credible do those adjustments seem?

Decision-makers can learn from experience of similar projects. For instance, where the stages of a complex project are tightly interlinked, even a short disruption can have far-reaching ramifications if those affected are unable to easily rearrange their schedules. Those who approve plans should ask why this project is expected to run more smoothly than previous ones. Using outside expertise can also help to keep plans realistic.

Before projects leave the drawing board, the following questions should be answered:

- What will this project achieve?
- How can we be sure?
- Why is it necessary?
- How will that achievement be realised?
- What other ways are there of achieving those objectives?

These questions may seem obvious, but as discussed in Chapter 3, white elephants get built because solutions have a habit of latching on to problems. For instance, TAURUS was sustained by the myth that the project was essential to the City of London's continued pre-eminence as a financial centre. Yet by itself, TAURUS achieved nothing. It merely paved the way for faster settlement. This objective could have been achieved simply through banks and other stakeholders changing their systems. There was no need for an expensive IT-based solution. Yet few dared to question TAURUS publicly until the project was cancelled. The time to ask whether a project is really necessary is when it is in embryo – not when it is falling apart.

Problems should be framed in as many different ways as possible. For example, instead of expressing a decision as a choice between losing market share and overpaying for an acquisition (negative framing), broaden the options. What other ways are there of expanding market share? Similarly, if the bottle is perceived to be half empty, imagine it as half-full.

Recognising and reacting to the larger signs

Decision-makers should normally declare failure when feedback consistently suggests that important expectations are unlikely to be met. The risks of escalation are heightened if expectations are fuzzy. Fuzzy expectations make failure harder to recognise. This means that decisions about ending a project are open to political contest. The lesson is simple: it must be clear from the start what a project is expected to achieve and how the achievements will be measured.

Most projects slip one day at a time. Research has shown that we are more sensitive to the latest small setback (a few thousand dollars here, a week or two's delay there) than the total amount of slippage. Spotting when things are going adrift is much easier when there are clear milestones and targets and progress is tracked against them. Monitoring the gap between plans and reality makes the total slippage obvious and undeniable.

It can be wise to reinvest in a doubtful project to give it every chance of success. Paris Disneyland got off to a poor start but has become an important tourist attraction. Oil is becoming harder and more expensive to find but the economics still work. The fact that initial results disappoint is not by itself a reason to quit. Even so, decision-makers should protect themselves by setting limits and quitting points. Moreover, when those limits are reached, pull the plug – unless there is a good reason to do otherwise. Setting limits and quitting points is one of the most effective damage-limitation means of curbing escalation. But the strategy only works if decision-makers stick to them.

With bad news, it is safest to assume that there is no smoke without fire. Then look for the fire. Seek out contradictory data. Go in search of more. Broaden information channels by speaking directly to people you would not normally consult in person. Pay particular attention to what juniors say. Their views are often filtered out of the chain of communications if they contradict the ruling myth. If you approach them directly, you may discover that they are refreshingly honest.

Look to the future

The amount of money invested in a venture is irrelevant: what matters are future costs and benefits. For instance, a film has a budget of $200m. Cost overruns mean that another $150m is needed to complete the work. Box-office returns are expected to net $200m. Since a partly completed film is worthless, the calculation is spending $150m in order to realise $200m. As marginal revenues exceed marginal costs, in theory, the film is worth completing even though it means investing $350m to earn $200m.

In an influential paper, "Dollars, sense and sunk costs", Gregory Northcraft and Gerrit Wolf, both formerly professors at the University of Arizona, contradict the sunk costs rule.[8] They argue that some projects are worth completing despite significant cost overruns and/ or revenue shortfalls. Their starting point is that few projects live up to the extravagant claims that were made for them at the outset. Even if expectations are not fully met, a project may be worth continuing on a cost/benefit basis. More specifically, where:

- the benefits are sufficiently large, or
- the project is worth completing despite setbacks, or
- the project is vital, or
- there is no better alternative.

If the benefits are sufficiently high, persistence may make sense. For instance, a $1 bet offering a 1/1,000 chance of winning $100,000 is an attractive proposition even though the probability of incurring 100 failures is over 90%. Similarly, hybrid cars may repay further research and development even though initial sales have been disappointing. This is because if the technology could be improved sufficiently, the pay-off could be huge. In other words, if the prospective pay-off is big enough, it may be worth persisting even though we accumulate failure after failure.

Thus a failed bet is irrelevant in deciding whether to buy another lottery ticket. This is because the probability of winning is known and each draw is independent of the last. Failure says nothing about what might happen in the future. Conversely, in oil exploration, failure – that is, dry wells – may be highly indicative of future prospects. For instance, in certain terrain one dry well might mean the likelihood of striking oil falls to 51%; with two dry wells it falls to 19%. In other words, decisions about whether to persist or quit should reflect the intelligence contained in failure, not the failure itself.

Some projects are commissioned not because they are cost-effective, but because they are effective. For example, Scotland's new Forth Road Bridge will be built despite the severe economic downturn as the project is crucial to Scotland's economy. The old bridge has become so worn that in a few years it will no longer be able to carry lorry traffic. Similarly, if a project involves manufacturing weapons to counter an extreme threat, or developing a vaccine against a potentially lethal epidemic, or injecting billions of dollars to support a tottering bank, outcomes are all-important. The fact that it is going to cost more than expected is irrelevant or at least secondary.

Where cost-effectiveness does matter, decisions about whether to quit or continue should reflect the financial structure of the project. Financial structure refers to the size of the cost overrun and/or what the revenue shortfall is likely to be and the timing of expected returns. The next task, according to Northcraft and Wolf, is to calculate the so-called "region of rationality" – that is, the economically sustainable gap between intended and realised costs and revenues over time, allowing for future costs and future benefits. The wider it is, the greater the room for manoeuvre.

Calculating the region of rationality is beyond the scope of this book as it requires an accountant. Generally, say Northcraft and Wolf, the more invested in a project early on, and the larger and later the prospective pay-off, the wiser it is to persist. In other words, the optimal number of investments:

- increases with pay-off;
- decreases with investment cost;
- increases with the likelihood of success.

For instance, the wastewater treatment plant in the desert city of Fallujah was planned as a showpiece for the rebuilding of Iraq by introducing Western standards of sanitation. The potential pay-off was therefore high as good sanitation is a fundamental prerequisite of economic and social development. By 2009, however, the cost had tripled from the original $100m. The project was three years behind schedule. Moreover, there was no money left to connect homes to the main sewer lines. Even if the money could be found, there was no guarantee of success because the electricity supply to the pumps and purification tanks was not reliable. All in all, based on the aforementioned criteria, it seems like a marginal project.

Yet before abandoning a project, alternative investment opportunities should be examined. If the returns are inferior, persistence with the existing project may be justified despite cost overruns and/or benefit shortfalls that would otherwise be deemed fatal. The UK's NHS patient record system was already over five years behind schedule when it created chaos in a pilot test in a hospital. The lesson is that although in theory a project fails when expectations cannot be met, in practice real failure occurs when support is withdrawn. In other words, part of the role of project managers is to maintain support for the project. They may do this by stressing the benefits, exaggerating progress and understating the difficulties.

Allowing for fallibility

In practice assessing future costs and benefits may not be as easy as it sounds. First, rather than looking to the future, decision-makers may be obsessed with justifying past decisions. For instance, research has shown that decision-makers who were responsible for initiating a faltering project tended to submit more requests for data vindicating their original decision than those who merely inherited the project.

Second, revised estimates are open to the same anchoring and over-optimism slants as the originals. TAURUS was nearly cancelled 18 months into construction when serious problems emerged with its design and there were unexpected legal complexities in removing paper from the system. After a comprehensive review, the London Stock Exchange decided to persist despite huge cost overruns and delays. But what did that decision rest upon? When the LSE board quizzed Peter Rawlins, the chief executive, about whether he was satisfied with the new projected budgets and timescales, he replied:[7]

> I said that provided the government enacted legislation within the promised timescale, provided there were no further changes to the project, and provided there were no more problems with the technology, then yes, I was content. But, big provisos.

As we now know, those provisos never materialised. Yet the case for continuance based on future costs and benefits seemed entirely rational.

When calculating the region of rationality, decision-makers should allow a big margin for error. For example, in early 1993, three years into construction, the City of London learned that TAURUS would take another three years to finish and cost another £90m. A member of the project's monitoring group said, "Well, maybe that's four years and £120m. There isn't that amount of value in the project. There never was. That decision makes itself." It was probably a wise judgment.

Besides, what matters is not what has been done but what remains to be done. The Fallujah sewer project has been scaled down to serve only the city centre. But as the Iraqi government has refused to pay the $10,000 per household connection cost, it may never work. The government suggested instead that householders should brave potentially lethal fumes and do the connecting themselves. However, there is also a question mark over the construction of the principal sewer pipe, as effluent could surge back into residents' homes. Given these unresolved challenges, the balance tilts towards abandonment. A project may be 80% complete. But this statistic can be highly misleading, particularly if the hardest part of construction lies ahead – for example, if novel technology is to be introduced right at the end.

Going for it

Another danger with sunk costs is that they can produce over-optimism. In an experiment two groups of people studied a plan to build an aircraft undetectable by radar. Each group was then asked to estimate the probability of successful completion. Group 1 was told that the project was still at an early stage of development and that little money had been invested in it. Group 2 was told that that millions of dollars had already been invested in constructing the aircraft. Group 2 were much more optimistic about the chances of success even though they had identical information about the project.

By implementing careful controls over the experiments, the researchers established that optimism was a direct consequence of sunk costs. This may explain why project planners in Iraq insist that the core objectives of the sewer scheme can still be met. Their optimism may simply reflect the enormous investment that has been made in the project.

More extreme is when decision-makers decide that they may as well be hung for a sheep as a lamb (stealing sheep and lambs was once a capital offence in Britain). In investment banking this is known as "traders' option". If traders know they will be sacked for poor returns, they have nothing to lose by making ever more reckless bets in an effort to trade their way back to profit. Such may be the cost of managing by fear.

Letting it lie

As a tree falls, says the proverb, so shall it lie. Some losses are best just accepted. Yet because losses weigh more heavily than gains (the pleasure of finding $1 is less than the pain of losing $1), the temptation is to recoup them at all costs. BAA set a much wiser example when the Heathrow Express project was severely disrupted after one of the main tunnels collapsed in October 1994. The collapse was one of the worst civil-engineering disasters in history. Yet instead of suing the contractor, Balfour Beatty, for breach of contract, BAA worked with it to retrieve the project. By looking to the future, the damage was limited as the project achieved its new start date. Moral: don't get mad, don't get even; get what you want.

HP should have followed BAA's example when its former chief executive, Mark Hurd, took a job with Oracle. Instead, HP immediately served a writ. It was a mistake because although HP had sacked Hurd, the industry relies a lot on co-operation between firms. Suing people is not conducive to co-operation. Although the decision was reversed, the damage was done. Moral: think twice before acting. There is always a tomorrow.

The role of budgets

Budget setting can stop projects from spiralling out of control. For example, in some high-risk industries such as pharmaceuticals, research and development is funded one stage at a time. New projects must undergo rigorous reassessment at every stage of the process before funding is renewed. Moreover, the expectation is that many will be culled.

A word of caution: research has shown that budgeting can lead to economically sound projects being curtailed. This is because decision-makers are often reluctant to reinvest if the budget is either spent or almost spent. This is irrational because budget depletion is what accountants call a "non-informative loss". In other words, budget depletion simply means that a certain amount of money has been spent. It says nothing about the state of the project and whether it is still worth completing. The budget may simply have been insufficient to begin with. EMI planned to record all Haydn's symphonies. But it abandoned the project when it reached number 67. It probably regretted the decision, as there are few recordings of the complete set. Did EMI simply under-budget and throw away a valuable opportunity as a result? Depletion alone should never be a reason to stop a project. If the cupboard is bare, firms should redirect resources.

Similarly, spiralling costs do not necessarily mean that a project is ill conceived. They may tell decision-makers nothing except that the project is turning out to be more expensive than forecast. Yet experiments have shown that even sophisticated decision-makers find it hard to distinguish informative losses from non-informative ones. They are just as likely to stop investing as budgets are exhausted, even though they are not learning from failure. It is unclear why. Perhaps having experienced mounting losses, decision-makers become wary of sacrificing too much to reach their goal.

We budget time as well as money. More specifically, psychologists believe that decision-makers are more likely to invest time to recoup money rather than money to recoup money, and money to recoup time rather than time to recoup time.

In practice, time is usually more important than money. For instance, the decision to abandon TAURUS was not about money. It was the prospect of waiting at least another three years. A member of the project-monitoring group said:

> The City could have swallowed the money bit. They would have said, "OK, there is an overspend of £100m – lets fight about who is going to fund that because we see the benefits coming through." It was the time that killed them all.

Stepping back

It is also important to stand back and ask why a project is failing. This may seem an obvious point to make. But when project teams are under pressure to deliver, they can become so absorbed in meeting the next deadline that they never stop to question whether the project is still feasible and worth completing. For example, it may be possible to scale down a failing project, or divide it into smaller, more manageable projects.

To change the project, it may be necessary to change the project manager. Dedicated managers can invest so much of themselves in a project that their judgment becomes clouded. They may reach a point where they can no longer see the wood for the trees.

If it is necessary to end a project, it is important to act swiftly and decisively. There should be no room for doubt and no indecision. The case for closure must be clear, reasoned and rock solid. Even then, project managers may insist that that they know how to make the project work, given just a little more money and a little more time. It is tempting to believe them. This is why escalation is a ubiquitous problem.

9 Decisionless decisions: the continuity trap

"We've travelled too far, and our momentum has taken over; we move idly towards eternity, without possibility of reprieve or hope of explanation."

Tom Stoppard, *Rosencrantz and Guildenstern are Dead*, Act 3

WHEN THE TELEPHONE FIRST ARRIVED AT FRESHFIELDS (now Freshfields Bruckhaus Deringer), a law firm, it was lodged in the basement. Partners decreed that the newfangled device was for making appointments only. On no account was it to be used to discuss clients' business. So the pressure for change had been accepted but the pressure for continuity remained strong. This is often the case, but if these conflicting pressures are well managed, firms can usually deal with threats and opportunities in a timely fashion, without becoming destabilised.

When the desire for continuity prevails over pressure for change, firms can end up "drifting idly towards eternity" and eventually die. In the 1950s, the United States led the world in steel production but lost out to Japan. Research in Motion, makers of the innovative BlackBerry device, took so long to produce a tablet computer that in 2011 the *Wall Street Journal* suggested the firm be renamed "Research in Slow Motion". Sony might have had a happier history if it had cut production of its flat-screen televisions sooner than it did, or even exited the business altogether. Diageo would have done better if it had linked its Johnny Walker whisky to Formula 1 racing sooner, instead of persisting for so long with the unfashionable association with tartan and other things Scottish.

Many more examples can be cited. Although the Apple iPhone

is designed in the United States, most of the components are made in Asia. Whereas Apple profits hugely from controlling iTunes and other software applications, the Asian component manufacturers' profit margin is less than 5%. Why do these manufacturers not switch to more profitable lines of activity? Nokia was once a world leader in mobile phones. Why did it not move into the more profitable smartphone market much earlier? Similarly, why was Sony slow to address an unprofitable line of activity?

The previous chapter focused on how and why firms can become caught up in a spiral of escalating commitment and end up "throwing good money after bad". This chapter explores a different form of "lock-in" known as entrapment. Entrapment is more insidious than escalation. This is because it does not require a deliberate decision to reinvest resources in an economically poor line of activity. Entrapment happens mainly through the simple passage of time. Yet "lock-in" need not be inevitable, provided decision-makers recognise two things. One is that the passage of time is not without cost. The second is that doing nothing is itself a decision with potentially far-reaching consequences.

Decisionless decisions

Investment decisions should reflect future costs and benefits. This means we should change track if an opportunity offering a better return becomes available even if it means abandoning a successful venture. Merchant bankers were originally merchants who used their good name to guarantee the debts of lesser merchants. They discovered that they could earn more money from this sideline than from trade itself. So even though they were successful merchants, they gradually gave up that occupation to become full-time bankers. More recently, when Tullow Oil abandoned expensive North Sea explorations to pursue new opportunities in Uganda and Ghana, including the Jubilee field (see page 8), the result was an 827% rise in share price and an entry to the FTSE 100 index. Tullow's willingness to redirect resources in a timely manner shows what can happen when firms follow economic principles.

In practice, however, changing track may be easier said than done because of "side-bets", or incidental investments. Side-bets are "decisionless decisions" that can unintentionally bind us to economically poor lines of activity. For example, new graduates seeking careers as commercial lawyers who take jobs in criminal law as a temporary expedient may, by the time an opportunity arises to change direction, decide to stay put. Having put a lot into developing an expertise, they discover that they are unwilling to undertake the huge task of retraining. This is an example of the side-bet of ease. Similarly, employees who acquire seniority rights such as protection from redundancy on a "last in, first out" basis may decide that the risk of moving is too great, even though it means forgoing a better-paid job. Entrepreneurs may enter business to get rich or as a response to redundancy. They then discover that they so enjoy the freedom and cachet of being self-employed that they are no longer willing to re-enter paid employment, even when they would be much better off financially. Although the side-bet of self-employment was incidental to the original decision to enter business, eventually it becomes the main reason for persistence.

Firms make side-bets too. For instance, incumbent suppliers frequently accumulate deep knowledge about a company, its needs, its plans and its people. Much of that knowledge is tacit. It cannot be codified and passed on to another supplier. Moreover, relationships develop and become stabilised. If a supplier is dropped, the slow process of knowledge transfer and building of mutual trust and confidence has to start all over again. This may explain why over 65% of contracts are renewed, even though the suppliers are judged to be indifferent. Although firms know that persistence is economically suboptimal, the costs of inconsistency are too high.

Waiting for "lock-in"

Whereas escalation is driven by irrational impulses, entrapment starts with decisions that were entirely rational to begin with. Yet eventually persistence can only make things worse. "Bad" can never turn to "good". For instance, the longer we are kept "on hold" on the telephone, the more exasperating and in many instances more expensive waiting becomes. Yet since giving up doesn't mean the process will be quicker when you call again, the pressure to persist increases with the passage of time – particularly if we are led to believe that we are next in line to speak to an operator. How long do we wait?

To see what would happen, an experiment was conducted which involved solving a crossword puzzle for an $8 prize.[1] The maximum time allowed for the task was 13 minutes. The size of the prize fell over time. Moreover, the puzzle was designed to be almost impossible to solve without the aid of a dictionary. Participants were told that they were first, second or third in line for this valuable resource. In other words, the experiment was designed so that waiting time was experienced both as an investment and an expense. Time spent waiting for the dictionary was an investment in that the sooner the dictionary arrived, the bigger the prize. Yet elapsed time was also experienced as an expense because the longer participants waited for the dictionary, the less they stood to win. Participants were divided into two groups. Those in group 1 had "real-time" charts depicting the precise rate at which the cash prize was declining. Those in group 2 were deprived of this information. In addition, for some participants, the value of the prize declined slowly; for others it declined more rapidly. All participants were free to stop the game and take the $2.40 stake money lying on the desk – but only if they acted during the first three minutes. After that time, the value of the stake money also declined.

In fact, there was no dictionary. Yet 87% of participants stayed beyond the three-minute deadline when they could have left with a small profit. More than half remained beyond breakeven point, that is, where the prize equalled the $2.40 consolation prize. A subsequent debriefing revealed that the longer participants waited, the sillier it seemed to give up. Eventually, of course, participants could no longer hope to complete the crossword without the dictionary so they decided that they had no choice but to continue waiting. We can infer from this experiment that decision-makers are more likely to succumb to "lock-in" when they fail to consider what persistence might eventually cost them.

Some kinds of potentially costly waiting are hard to avoid. For example, when a firm makes a job offer, the successful candidate may need time to think things over. Should the person subsequently decline the appointment, however, other acceptable candidates may have found jobs elsewhere. So the firm ends up having to re-advertise the post. Europe's car industry is in the doldrums with more cars than customers. Firms like Renault and GM should shift even more production to low-cost countries like Turkey. But cutting capacity is expensive. For example, if GM closed Opel-Vauxhall, the redundancy costs for the 40,000 workers would be about €8 billion. It is not a decision to be taken lightly. But putting it off may just make things worse.

Doing nothing is not an option

Entrapment can start because the cost of not doing something is initially minuscule. To illustrate the point let's start with a simple example. Jim (a pseudonym) is a highly successful fishmonger yet he almost let the business slip through his hands. It was a conventional wet-fish business with about 14 lines: cod, haddock, plaice, and so on. Jim went on holiday leaving his daughter in charge. She had long been urging him to expand the range. Jim resisted because of the cost. When he returned from holiday, he was horrified to find that his daughter had bought boxes of exotic fish such as bass, sea bream and John Dory. However, far from being a disaster, the shop now sells mainly exotic fish. If it had stuck to conventional lines, the business would have survived for a while, but eventually it would no longer be viable.

Citigroup suffered the biggest subprime losses of all of the American universal banks, thanks to its determination to close the gap between itself and other leading investment banks, notably Goldman Sachs. If the "Jims" of Goldman Sachs had had their way in the early 1990s, the firm might not have been such an enviable force to reckon with. In December 1990 Steve Friedman and Bob Rubin were named senior partners and co-chairmen of the management committee. Their ambitious vision involved expanding the firm to offer a full range of expertise, allowing it to compete with the biggest investment banks and offer new services. Many of the partners opposed the idea, particularly as its boutique model had served the firm well.

Goldman Sachs, with 6,500 employees, was highly successful, and the partnership was by its nature conservative. After a decade of astounding prosperity, the impetus for change was low. But in Friedman's view:[2]

> We were moving too slowly, or not at all, to face some serious competitive threats ... and with too much self-satisfaction. Too many things were on autopilot and were not re-examined. If we waited to fix them it might get too late.

The firm could have continued as it was for a while. Yet, as the partners recognised, it would inevitably decline and eventually reach a point of no return. Similarly, after more than a century of owning De Beers, the Oppenheimer family decided, apparently reluctantly, to sell a controlling stake to Anglo American. Yet the decision may well have been timely given the sale price of $5.1 billion. De Beers may be the world's biggest diamond miner and the industry leader today. But who knows what the future may hold? Firms' fortunes are subject to sudden and dramatic shifts. Sometimes it is best to take the money and run.

When a business is thriving, resource-allocation decisions are likely to be positively framed. Continuity (whether it involves fish, financial contracts or something else) usually means a definite gain, whereas change involves risk. It could turn out to be a disaster. Consequently, when things are going well, decision-makers may well be risk averse. Being content with the proverbial bird in the hand is seen as a better course of action than pursuing the two in the bush. What firms may forget is that in business, existing gains are transient. In 2006 shares in Hon Hai were trading at HK$27. In 2012 they were trading below $4. Nokia's ascendancy reflected the firm's ability to design and produce attractive, easy-to-use handsets cheaply. Yet these advantages became a liability when the industry moved towards providing software and data services. Nokia had configured the company to produce handsets for conversation and text messaging – not smartphones. It was good while it lasted, but not once the game had changed. Many firms and even whole industries have never recovered from game-changing developments: the internet has transformed retailing; low-cost airlines shook up the big carriers; and the music industry made a huge error when it failed to appreciate the threat of digital technology to its business model.

Comfort zones and sacred cows

Although prospect theory may explain why successful firms are sometimes slow to heed environmental change and as a result succumb to entrapment, faltering firms are often surprisingly slow to respond to obvious environmental threats. The American steel industry made the mistake of clinging to open hearth technology. This involves burning excess carbon and other impurities out of pig iron to produce steel. It is a slow process. As cheap pure oxygen became available and furnaces improved, basic oxygen technology began to replace open hearth. Japan embraced basic oxygen technology from the start. It cut refining time from 6–10 hours to 40 minutes, capital costs by a half and operating costs by a third. Not only did open hearth technology persist in the United States for another 20 years, but the industry also invested more money in it, adding oxygen lances and enlarging hearths. It is true that replacement costs were high, but this was not the only reason for persisting with obsolete technology. American manufacturers understood open hearth and felt at ease with it.

More recently, Steve Eastbrook, president and chief executive of McDonald's UK, admitted that the chain should have responded sooner to changing consumer preferences for healthy eating. "The business had stalled ... We hadn't done a good enough job of reacting to some of the signals we were getting out there," he said. Again, firms, like individuals, have their comfort zones and they are often reluctant to venture beyond them.

The dangers of lock-in to an economically poor line of activity are thought to be heightened if that activity becomes identified with the values and purposes of the firm. In the days of mechanical calculating machines, Facit, a firm based in the United States, built a formidable reputation for its comptometers (key-driven calculators). Facit knew everything there was to know about the business. Its record of quality and customer service was unimpeachable. When electronic calculators first appeared, Facit decided that its customers would be slow to abandon tried and tested technology. As plummeting sales contradicted that belief, Facit sold its profitable typewriter business to support comptometers, as it saw them as its core business. When Chrysler ran into financial difficulties, it jettisoned many of its Dodge and Jeep models even though they were strongly identified with the company. It was a wise move. Similarly, Daimler was probably wise to kill off the prestigious Maybach after years of poor sales. Since the car's relaunch in 2002, only about 200 a year had been sold. In comparison, 2,711 Rolls-Royces and 5,000 Bentleys were sold in 2011 alone – suggesting that the Maybach had captured only a fraction of the main luxury car market. In contrast, Sony, the inventor of portable music, continued to use up resources marketing the famous Walkman long after digital technology appeared.

Sacred cows suck resources from more profitable lines of activity. HP's chief executive, Mark Hurd, cut R&D budgets (see Chapter 6). Challenging the hitherto sacrosanct stimulated new thinking within HP. Executives began to openly question whether the firm should continue to be so heavily dependent upon innovation and low-margin personal computers. That debate prompted HP to find a new strategic direction. The firm has since become more solutions and service oriented, as shown, for example, by the acquisition of EDS. It could well be that but for those changes, HP might eventually have passed into history along with other household names such as Pullman and Singer. Even so, the firm is by no means out of danger. Its TouchPad tablet was an embarrassing failure. HP halted production only weeks after the product was launched following poor sales. Momentum is like reputation: that is, easily lost and hard to regain.

The cost of entrapment

"What can be accounted for by fewer assumptions is explained in vain by more," said William of Ockham (c1280–1349), a Franciscan friar and philosopher. William's observation has become the guiding precept of theory building for scientists and social scientists alike. It is an argument for parsimony. If an outcome can be explained by one overarching cause, there is no need to invoke multiple sub-causes because the additions yield no extra explanatory power. They merely complicate things, making the theory less useful. Is there a simple, that is, parsimonious explanation for entrapment?

The phantom dictionary experiment shows that those who believed they were first in line for this non-existent resource waited the longest. Waiting times were even longer if participants had no pay-off charts, and when the value of the prize declined slowly rather than rapidly. In a sequel experiment participants received an initial stake of $4 and the promise of an additional $2 prize. Participants were divided into two groups. Those in one group had to actively decide to remain in the game; unless they took a clear decision to continue, they were automatically disqualified from winning the prize. In contrast, those in the other group remained in the game automatically unless they decided to quit. All participants were told:

> *If you decide to go for the jackpot, the experimenter will set the counter in motion until it reaches the number 20, or until the tone sounds – whichever comes first. If the tone has not sounded by the time the counter reaches 20, there will be a short pause and a decision point. During this time, you must decide what you would like to do.*

As in the phantom dictionary experiment, the tone never sounded. Participants were therefore forced to decide every 20 units whether to continue or quit. As a result, participants who needed to make only a passive decision to stay in the game tended to remain longer than those who had to make an active decision to persist. They also incurred bigger losses.

Taken together, the two experiments suggest (parsimoniously) that entrapment is most likely to happen in situations where the costs of persistence are obscured. This implies that lock-in is avoidable provided decision-makers keep careful account of what it is costing them to carry on. In practice, this may be harder than it sounds. For instance, by the time the American F-35 Joint Strike Fighter comes into service in 2016 (six years late and hugely over budget) it is likely that drones (unmanned aircraft) will be more useful. The Pentagon knows exactly what persistence with the $382 billion project is costing. Yet cancelling the programme would be difficult and risky if drones fail to fulfil their promise.

Entrapment may happen by accident. Yet decision-makers are not necessarily powerless to prevent it. As noted earlier, we are more likely to persist in an economically suboptimal activity when the decision to remain can be made passively. We can infer from this that the likelihood of lock-in is heightened by the absence of a crisis. Whether a business involves fish, financial contracts or fast food, a crisis forces decision-makers to confront their options. The trouble is that by the time a crisis erupts it is often too late, as the spiral of decline has become irreversible. One way of countering this danger is to ensure that important decisions have to be made actively. For example, rules may limit the number of times contracts can be awarded to the same supplier. It may also be helpful to review suppliers' performance frequently – particularly if external experts conduct the review.

It is important to monitor what persistence is costing. Moreover, as with escalation scenarios (see Chapter 8), decision-makers should set limits on how long they are prepared to wait. Moreover, they should quit when those limits are reached. Those who succumb to the temptation to wait just a little longer may suffer a similar fate to those who wait too long. They reach a point where there it is too late to try and solve the puzzle without the aid of a dictionary. Waiting begets waiting.

Trapped by human nature

Even if costs are monitored and even if it is plainly in our interests to do so, we may still be reluctant to change course. Such reluctance arises from our innate preference as human beings for the status quo. More specifically we tend to:

- discount the future;
- prefer inaction to action;
- prefer mistakes of omission to mistakes of commission; and
- prefer what we have, even though we could have something better.

Discounting the future refers to our tendency to behave as if the future will never arrive. For instance, research has shown that an immediate gain of $10,000 is often preferable to a gain of $12,000 in a year's time, even though the second option is much more valuable. Our innate preference for inaction over action means that we prefer solutions that "do no harm". This may be a sound precept for practising medicine, but in business it results in shunning decisions that involve a small risk of harm but can yield big benefits. For example, Camelot, a UK-based firm that runs the National Lottery, now recognises that it was too slow to introduce online playing for fear of internet fraud. Camelot was too cautious – perhaps too influenced by vivid images of cyber-crime. Similarly, we tend to worry more about making mistakes than the potential costs of doing nothing. For example, some outsourcing decisions are extremely expensive to reverse. Yet rather than take the risk of an outsourced activity failing and needing to be brought back in-house, firms fail to grasp the nettle. Therefore they end up incurring needless cost. Similarly, we tend to cling to what we have (including obsolete technology and indifferent suppliers) when we could easily have something better.

We also tend to attach more weight to losses than gains. In other words, the pain of losing $100 is much more acute than the pleasure experienced in finding $100. Again, this means we are likely to shun decisions involving an initial loss but an overall gain. For instance, switching suppliers is usually disruptive. But in the longer term, the disruption may be well worth it. Likewise, UBS could have taken control and shifted course by unloading or at least freezing potentially problematic subprime positions in a timely fashion (see page 34). Had it done so, it would not have incurred such huge losses. As the Buddha says, don't hold onto anything – meaning let go of emotional attachments to people and material goods. It is also a good mantra for business strategies that have outlived their usefulness.

Persistence with an economically poor line of activity can also be driven by sheer force of habit. Habit implies there is no learning experience. Decision-makers merely execute their routines. The attraction of habit is that it enables us to act unreflectively. Instead of thinking about the opportunity costs of continuity, we carry on doing what we have always done. Moreover, when we do what we have always done, we learn little that is new.

Decision-makers may go through a process of reducing their emotional commitment before they can bring themselves to close a failing venture. A bigger danger is procrastination. To procrastinate is to have an intention but fail to carry it out. It involves postponement of behaviour that is emotionally unappealing, but will lead to positive outcomes. At least a process of anticipatory grieving reduces the psychological pain of quitting. For example, entrepreneurs who grieve for a failed business may find it easier to start again than those who do not grieve. In contrast, procrastination achieves nothing except temporary psychological safety – usually at the expense of deeper entanglement. Would-be procrastinators should remember Queen Elizabeth I's alleged dying murmur: "All my possessions for a moment of time." As the dying queen recognised, time is worth much more than money. Money can be replaced. A moment of elapsed time is gone forever. We cannot recall the last few seconds, let alone the years that might have been better spent.

In summary, we may be tempted to delay changes that must be made sooner or later, even though we know that by making them later those changes come at greater cost. Maybe that was why Churchill was so keen on "action this day".

Procrastinators may be motivated by fear of regret. Psychologists believe that people are regret averse, and so one way of avoiding entrapment is to leave no place for regrets. This often means that they end up doing nothing.

Another way of escaping from inaction traps may be to start with the low-hanging fruit – the quick wins, in other words. Tom Peters, a business writer, calls it the "little big things", that is, the small almost effortless changes that make a big difference. For example, making a three-minute phone call about a possible collaboration or merger with another firm that has been on the "to do" list for weeks or even months.[3] As a Chinese proverb says, a journey of a thousand miles begins with a single step.

But it has to be the right step. Military doctrine holds that in war, the boldest moves are the safest. It is good maxim for business provided boldness is combined with caution. For example, despite its distinguished history, by the early 1990s IBM was in poor shape. IBM triggered a renaissance with the advent of IBM Blue in the late 1990s. Instead of doing the obvious by entering the mainstream but crowded PC market, IBM focused on making high-end machines for scientists and professionals. The strategy was bold because it staked everything on a small segment of the market being willing to pay for supercomputing. It was cautious because IBM did not stray from its core expertise. And it worked.

10 Risk a little, gain a lot: options thinking

"Good management is not just about making the right decisions. It is about making the right decision at the right time."

Anon

THALES OF MILETUS, a Greek philosopher, read his tealeaves. He divined that the olive harvest would be bountiful. Next he bought the right (but not the obligation) to rent olive presses at normal rates come harvest time. The forecast was correct. Olive growers were desperate for pressing capacity. Thales made a fortune by subletting the olive presses for an extortionate sum, demonstrating just how good an investment an "option" can be.[1]

This chapter explores the role of options.[2] Options can be a useful tool in preventing escalation and entrapment, with options theory working on the principle that small failures are preferable to large ones. Much has been said in this book about undue risk-taking and failure on a grand scale. Options, by contrast, are about taking affordable risks that help avoid damaging losses and may lead to substantial gains.

Falling forwards

An option is a toehold investment that confers the right but not the obligation to take action in the future. For example, the right to buy a quantity of oranges in three months' time at 10 cents each. If, in three months' time, oranges cost only 9 cents each, it makes no sense to exercise the option and the option holder loses the money paid for it. But if the price of has risen above 10 cents, the option is said to be "in the money" because the option holder can buy the oranges for less than the current market price. Buying an option buys certainty. The option holder has a guaranteed price ceiling for oranges three months hence, regardless of how much the market may have moved meanwhile. Options are bought because there is economic value in resolving uncertainty. This is why they are much used in commodities markets where prices for oil, metals and crops can be volatile. The same is true with currencies. For example, a European firm contracting to buy something priced in dollars may protect itself from adverse exchange-rate fluctuations by buying an option to buy the requisite amount of dollars at the time the purchase price will be due.

In other words, options theory assumes that the ability to change course in the light of new information is valuable.[3] Indeed, the alternative may be costly lock-in (see Chapters 8 and 9 on escalation and entrapment). For instance, in a business start-up there are no guarantees of success. It pays to be cautious and not overinvest in factory buildings and the like. But if the venture succeeds, the factory building may soon be too small. The firm may wish it had built a bigger factory. But that would have exposed it to additional risk. Buying land adjacent to the factory (with requisite building permissions) enables the firm to expand if the venture prospers. If the venture is not as successful as hoped, the land is not built on. Any loss is confined to the purchase of the land less any resale value. It is known as falling forwards rather than backwards.

Options are a style of thinking, and in terms of strategic choices, a firm's resources, that is, its capabilities, knowledge and assets, can be thought of as a storehouse of options. Whereas decision-making usually focuses on avoiding uncertainty, in contrast options thinking focuses on embracing uncertainty. For instance, in 2009, Shell (with Petronas of Malaysia) secured a contract to develop the Majnoon field in southern Iraq, one of the biggest oilfields in the world. By itself the venture is not expected to be particularly profitable. The attraction is that it represents a toehold investment in Iraq. That toehold might lead more lucrative possibilities when drilling licences for vast untapped tracts of desert eventually go on sale. In dealing with market uncertainties, HP decided to incorporate all four industry standards into the design of its printers rather than guess which type of input slot was likely to prove most popular and risk making a costly mistake. It meant higher production costs but the pay-off is increased consumer appeal. Any loss is limited to the extra manufacturing costs, whereas the gains are potentially unlimited.

The business options

The main options that companies have open to them are as follows:

- Immediate entry – advance a small amount in order to acquire the right to make a full commitment later.
- Immediate exit – make a full commitment but acquire the right to reverse it immediately.
- Delayed entry – acquire the right to enter the market later.
- Delayed exit – buy time before abandoning a project.
- Agility – the option to switch.
- Shadow – an option that emerges unexpectedly.
- Compound – an option within an option.
- Learning – paying to learn about uncertainty.
- Rainbow – getting the best of all worlds.

Immediate-entry options

An immediate-entry option involves advancing a small amount in order to acquire the right to purchase a full commitment later. When Woolworths UK closed, Frederick and David Barclay bought the name from the administrators. This small commitment enabled them subsequently to resurrect Woolworths online, via their Shop Direct group. Interns may not add much value to firms, but employing them can create a kind of delayed-entry option. That is, the firm gets the opportunity to talent spot without taking the risk of entering into an employment contract.

Immediate-exit options

An immediate-exit option involves making a full commitment but acquiring the right to reverse it immediately. For example, some software-development firms rely mainly on consultants. Although this is a more expensive solution than employing people, the attraction is flexibility. For instance, if a contract is cancelled, the firm can immediately shed surplus labour.

Delayed-entry options

Delayed-entry options occur when decision-makers purchase the right to enter the market later. An oil-exploration company may acquire land and a drilling licence and locate the oil, but postpone production until the price of oil rises sufficiently. Similarly, speculative builders may buy land cheaply during a recession and build on it only if property prices rise above a certain level. Delayed-entry options are useful where entering the market involves an expensive all-or-nothing commitment and/or where it is wise to wait for market or technological uncertainty to diminish before making a full commitment.

Firms may be able to resolve some uncertainties for themselves. BP discovered the Andrew field in the mid-1970s. It was small and difficult to drill, so BP left it until the mid-1990s. By then BP had developed the requisite technology and management techniques to make the venture profitable. Meanwhile, oil prices had risen markedly. Between 1990 and 1996, BP's market value rose from $18 billion to $30 billion, partly because the company used delayed-entry options in developing the Andrew field.

Instead of producing only petrol-driven cars, or taking the huge risk of producing only electric cars, firms such as Toyota and Volvo have opted for hybrids. Hybrids create the opportunity but not the obligation to eventually make a full commitment to electric propulsion should the technology be improved sufficiently. This is a form of delayed-entry option.

Another form is an option to expand. For instance, a firm may acquire additional plant and machinery. The intention is that the equipment normally stands idle but enables the firm to ramp up production if it needs to. BP learned about this form of option the hard way. In the early 1980s, it began developing the Magnus gas field. BP was too cautious about the field's potential and ended up building a platform that was too small, with no flexibility to increase production.

Conversely, there is the option to contract. Instead of buying a few big machines, firms may opt for lots of small ones. If demand falls, some of these can be kept idle without costing a fortune.

Delayed-exit options

Delayed-exit options allow decision-makers to buy time before abandoning a project. They are useful where exiting from a venture is expensive and virtually irreversible. For example, some diamond mines in Tanzania have been mothballed following the collapse of prices. It costs money to keep a mine in commission, but it is much cheaper than opening a new one should trade improve. Similarly, South Africa's best gold mines are now almost exhausted. Those that remain are very deep and very hot; even when ice is pumped in the ambient temperature is around 35°C, making them difficult and expensive to work. The gold is unlikely to be mined unless the price rises to a level that justifies the expense. Again, by keeping the mines in commission, that option exists. When Marks & Spencer refused to pay its suppliers more, Northern Foods, a UK supplier of ready meals, decided against persisting with an economically poor line of activity. Production at its Fenland Food Plant in Lincolnshire would cease. Yet rather than closing the factory altogether, Northern Foods decided to mothball it. Similarly, a power station may keep coal-fired plant in working order so as to have the option of bringing it back into commission if electricity prices suddenly rise. Delaying exit also saves the cost of removing redundant plant and equipment. Moreover, there is always the possibility that new technology becomes available that makes reopening a venture profitable.

But delayed-exit options may simply be perpetuating entrapment – for example, managers with a vested interest may insist on keeping a loss-making mine fully open on the pretext that it is the only way to retain a skilled labour force.

Agility options

Agility options include being able to switch production lines to different products as market demand changes and being able to switch suppliers. Some firms learned the value of agility options to their cost when the earthquake and tsunami that struck Japan in early 2011 destroyed supply chains. Suzuki had to halve production at its plant near Budapest after running out of components. Honda was forced to do the same at its Swindon plant in the UK. Mitsubishi Gas Chemical supplies about half the world's bismaleimide-triazine (BT) resin, which is used to make substrates that connect chips used in handsets to printed circuit boards. When the earthquake forced the company to suspend resin production indefinitely, handset manufacturers were left with few alternatives. In other words, a problem with no options is a failure of management.

Agility options are also relevant to career decisions. For instance, instead of choosing a degree in pharmacy or optometry, it may be better to start with a degree in medical sciences in order to acquire transferable knowledge. Then, as more information is accumulated about abilities, likes and dislikes, perhaps specialise at a later stage in the programme – or delay the choice until master's level. At master's level too it may be wise to keep options open. A general MBA may be more expensive than a specialist MBA in marketing or human resources management. The pay-off is more career options. Agility options can prevent entrapment because they allow the decision-maker to pursue the line of activity offering the highest returns – net of switching costs.

Shadow options

Shadow options emerge unexpectedly. Contrary to the corporate rhetoric, "people are our most valuable asset", a company's main value may reside in the options it has to grow and invest in the future, particularly in volatile and unpredictable industries such as biotechnology, electronics and telecommunications. In this view, managing a portfolio of options is the essence of strategy.

Shadow options allow strategy to emerge from opportunities that may not have been foreseen. To be more precise, shadow options arise when existing resources and capabilities give firms preferential access to opportunities. As discussed in Chapter 6, HTC originally made mobile phones for other companies. Eventually, its accumulated knowledge and expertise created the option to become a manufacturer in its own right. Similarly, Amazon's huge customer base, reputation and retail experience could eventually enable it to open "click-and-collect" high-street stores, should it choose to exercise that shadow option.

Firms that share knowledge and experience informally can create a shadow option to enter into a full merger. When JPMorgan bought a 50% stake in Cazenove in 2004 (its other suitor was Lehman Brothers), the auguries seemed doubtful, not least because of the cultural differences between the two firms manifested by the reluctance of Cazenove staff to carry BlackBerrys. Yet five years later, in November 2009, JPMorgan announced a full takeover, suggesting that the doubts have been resolved. The decision represents the exercise of a shadow option that has emerged from the collaboration.

Shadow options can also help firms avoid entrapment. Entrapment can happen when successful firms become risk averse and therefore reluctant to change direction before existing business models outlive their usefulness. Shadow options reduce the risks involved in changing direction. Its experience as a contractor reduced the risk for HTC. Similarly, collaboration between Cazenove and JPMorgan gave the eventual merger a better chance of success.

Even failure can create a shadow option. In the early 1980s attempts to create small handheld computers (PDAs) capable of reading handwritten text failed. The technology was later revived and incorporated into the commercially successful Palm Pilot and similar products. It is not just a matter of learning from failure, important though that may be. Preferential access comes from having the technology waiting in the wings.

Compound options

Compound options are an option or options in an option. They involve sequenced or staged investments. Making an initial investment gives the decision-maker the right but not the obligation to make a second investment, and so on. For instance, when developing new drugs, pharmaceutical companies may follow a staged process where if the initial investment is successful, the company has the option but not the obligation to reinvest.

Compound options are sometimes used strategically where it is not possible (or not wise) to reach point C from point A without first going through point B. An example is a large firm acquiring a small firm with proprietary technology. The acquirer gains the value of the company's existing operations and the option to subsequently market an improved version of the technology.

Learning options

Learning options involve paying to learn about uncertainty. For instance, a gas company holds a drilling licence for a field but has no reliable information about the extent of the reserves. It may therefore be wise to conduct exploratory research first. The information gleaned from the exercise can be used to make drilling more efficient. Plant and facilities can be built to the right size – not too big, not too small. To be more precise, learning options arise where decision-makers can pay to speed up the arrival of useful information. For example, designers may experiment with a small-scale model to see if their ideas are potentially robust before building large-scale prototypes. Learning options are valuable only if decisions can be changed in the light of new information.

Provided this condition is met, learning options can curb escalation. For instance, instead of opting for an all-out launch, firms may test a new product in a small geographical area. Afterwards, they can either abandon the product, or incorporate feedback into the design and marketing strategy. Pepsi Raw was a costly mistake (see Chapter 5). It could have been much worse but for Pepsi's learning option. Pepsi trialled the new drink in UK bars and then abandoned it. In short, paying to learn.

Rainbow options

Options can conflict. A rainbow option allows decision-makers to have their cake and eat it. More specifically, probing, say, a gas field to learn more about the state of reserves could destroy the option to postpone development of the field until gas prices rise. The standard, or rational, approach to this conflict is as follows. Compare the value of the information to be gained from a preliminary exploration with the value of deferring development. In other words, make an either/or decision. In contrast, a rainbow option involves conducting a partial exploration that allows the decision-maker to learn something about the reserves, while retaining the option of delaying full-scale production until prices rise sufficiently.

Other options ...

Many other options exist. Options to change course may minimise the risks of escalation by enabling a faltering project to be refocused. For example, the options available might be to assign an asset to a different purpose, or to change the scale of a project or abandon it with ease. And should a project be more successful than expected, there is always the pleasant surprise of the growth option.

... and a warning

Some options require the creation of infrastructure which may develop a life of its own, if only because of the effort involved in dismantling it. Thus some options can create entrapment or even escalation.

Value creation - and destruction

Broadly, investments that create options are more valuable than those that involve exercising them. Although R&D is fraught with risk, particularly in industries like pharmaceuticals and biotechnology, these activities generate more options than production. Similarly, so-called "wildcat" firms like Tullow and Heritage confine their activities to drilling for oil. They then sell their discoveries. The firms that buy these discoveries acquire an option. They can make a full investment now, or delay entry.

When making decisions, consider what options might be destroyed. Options are destroyed when investments are specific. Employees who develop skills that are firm specific have fewer options than employees with a broader skill set. A small consortium of retailers provides an example of the dangers of destroying your options. Having commissioned an IT-based stock-control system, they cancelled the contract when the project overran and bought a software package that seemed to meet most of their requirements. "That decision has been a millstone round their necks ever since," said a chief operating officer. "If they had only waited they could have had bespoke and something they could have sold to other retailers." Options are most valuable when uncertainty is high. The option to buy something at a fixed price in a year's time typically costs more than one for a month's time because the further in the future, the greater the uncertainty. Yet the biggest benefit of options thinking is profiting from uncertainty. Scenario planning recognises the existence of uncertainty but ignores the possible hidden value. This was Thales's genius.

Uncertainty can work against options. RCA was a world leader in liquid-crystal display technology in the early 1970s. But it abandoned its research programme because of the uncertainty surrounding the commercial future of the technology and the huge R&D costs. Had RCA persisted, the option created by developing liquid-crystal display capability might have proved extremely profitable given the advent of notebook and handheld computers.

Options thinking can also reveal hidden potential. For example, when analysed by conventional accounting methods such as net present value and economic profit, the Andrew field was a doubtful proposition. But when an options lens is applied, the opportunity may appear startlingly different.

An option may not be worth its cost. For instance, to attract good consultants, firms may need to guarantee them a fixed number of days' work a year. This concession dilutes the immediate exit option. Furthermore, regular employees may resent consultants, perceiving them to be better paid than themselves and/or as depriving them of overtime.

In a turbulent world, uncontrollable external forces may extinguish options. An option to expand may be useless if competitors move in first. Political turmoil could mean that Shell and Petronas's investment in Iraq never comes into the money. Shadow options may fizzle out unless the knowledge gained is properly documented. Besides, a shadow option has to be recognised before it can be struck. No reliable methodology exists for doing this. Decision-makers can rely only on their intuition and common sense.

Exercising decisions

Deciding whether to exercise a financial option is easy. There is a fixed expiry date. Moreover, the option is exercised only if the exercise price is below the market price. There is no uncertainty, so the decision makes itself. In contrast, exercising options requires careful judgment. There is still a lot of gold left in South Africa. But even though the price of gold has risen substantially since 2007, the mines have yet to be reopened. Conversely, how long should a mine be kept open amid falling commodity prices? Northern Foods used the mothballed plant to trial new equipment. Now that the trials are finished, how much longer should it pay to keep the plant in commission? There are no easy answers. Yet unless the decision-maker chooses the optimal time to strike, part or even all of the value of the option is lost.

To counter this problem, decision-makers should specify in advance the precise conditions under which an option will be exercised. They should also investigate carrying costs and ensure that the capability exists to support the option meanwhile.

Yet with options, uncertainty always lingers. In theory, efficient use of options depends on the time lag between the resolution of the uncertainty (where the trigger point is realised) and action. In practice, it may pay to delay exercising the option if making a full investment seems risky. For example, oil may reach a trigger price of, say, $100 a barrel, but there is no guarantee that it will remain at this level for long. Delaying exercising the option will allow the true trajectory to emerge. Thus rather than strike when an option is "in the money", it may be wise to wait until it is "deeper in the money".

The risk of killing a potentially valuable option may be heightened if the option is isolated from a firm's core competence. Xerox set up an autonomous R&D group that created options on PC networks and mouse interfaces. Yet it never exercised these options because PC networks and mouse interfaces were deemed to be too remote from the firm's core competences in marketing and xerography. The lesson is to be careful about using "goodness of fit" as a criterion for exercising an option.

The philosophy of war

Sun Tzu, an ancient Chinese military philosopher, suggests that in certain situations, commanders should cut off all lines of retreat for their own forces. The rationale for this potentially suicidal move is known as the single-option paradigm. This "all-or-nothing" approach may not be rational, but it can generate huge effort and commitment precisely because there is no alternative.

Closing thoughts

THE TASK OF DECISION-MAKING is complicated by the weaknesses and contradictions in our knowledge. Proverbs may be wise, but they also contradict one another. Fools rush in. Yet they who hesitate are lost.

Research should resolve such contradictions, not add to them. Yet Chapter 6 suggested that decisions shaped by endless political "shoving and hauling" can turn out well. In contrast, Chapter 7 showed that firms can fail most successfully; that is, they may act in ways that are entirely rational and purposeful but that turn out to be self-defeating. Chapter 6 suggested that the importance of leaders in influencing the fate of firms is overblown. Yet Chapter 5 showed that overbearing leaders can eclipse wiser counsels and lead their firms over a precipice. Chapter 1 warns that success can tempt decision-makers to take undue risks. In contrast, the main message of Chapter 9 is that successful firms can become too cautious. Why do our theories and research tie us in knots?

The role of theory is to explain and to predict. Medieval astronomers made superb predictions. For example, the window nearest the north transept of the medieval church of St Cross near Winchester in the UK is angled so that the sunlight falls on the church cross on only two days of the year. These are May 3rd, the feast of the Invention of the Cross, and September 14th, Holy Cross Day. The positioning of these windows suggests that medieval astronomers knew exactly where the sun would fall on two days of the year though they may not have known why.

Social sciences theories are nowhere near as accurate. Firms are so complex that research into human behaviour can seldom explain more than 20% of the observed variance. So our knowledge is shaky. For example, economists maintain that escalation theorists exaggerate. Economists say that escalation only happens in the private sector where there is less exposure to market discipline. To prove the point, two influential economists, Colin Camerer and Roberto Weber, reanalysed an important escalation study.[1] They expected that when more rigorous statistical controls were applied the escalation effect would disappear. To their surprise they discovered that although the effects were weaker than those observed in the original study, there was definitely escalation of commitment.

Indeed, escalation does not always happen as some projects are cancelled. A consulting engineer said:

> *If, say, a property developer is in it to make money, and if they realise they aren't going to make the $100,000 dollars per unit they had hoped to, they get out. Their spreadsheet tells them they have to.*

Even so, we are by no means home and dry. The consulting engineer is referring to situations that are clear cut. It is situations where there is a mixture of good news and bad news that provide the most fertile breeding ground for escalation. Decision dilemma theorists argue that all the social and psychological theories of escalation mentioned in Chapter 8 are superfluous because feedback is almost invariably equivocal to some extent. For instance, Cairn Energy, an Edinburgh-based group, abandoned drilling in Greenland after investing $1.2 billion in the venture. The project certainly bears the hallmarks of escalation, being dogged by technical problems and an invasion of Greenpeace protestors, which cost Cairn $4m a day. Yet failure is by no means clear. Drilling yielded encouraging seismic data. Moreover, Statoil of Norway was sufficiently interested to buy a stake in one of Cairn's exploration blocks. In other words, for all the ominous overtones, some of the ingredients of success are also present. Therefore, persistence ultimately reflects the time it takes for failure to become well and truly apparent. In this view, escalation should be seen as a normal business expense.

Behavioural theorists say that if social and psychological drivers are present, they should be accounted for. Even then, behavioural theorists disagree over whether escalation is primarily driven by fear of failure, or merely reflects how problems are expressed (framed) and can therefore occur regardless of personal responsibility for failure. If so, suggested measures to deal with escalation such as removing the project manager and rewarding managers on process rather than outcomes may not do any good. Conversely, it may be easier to get decision-makers to reframe problems than to remove their egos from the equation. Whatever the truth may be, our knowledge is much more flimsy than descriptions of experiments and so forth might suggest.

Some research findings are counter-intuitive. For instance, given the dangers of overconfidence, we might think that decision-makers are more attuned to opportunities than to threats. Yet in certain circumstances, the opposite may be true. Indeed, getting others to see opportunity instead of looming threat may be the secret of charismatic leadership.

Another problem is that we do not know enough about the limits of our theories. For instance, groups must be cohesive to function effectively. Yet Chapter 5 does not say when esprit de corps becomes groupthink. Chapter 4 points out that "lockdown" may be a double-edged response to severe threats, as both the survival and extinction capabilities of the firm are amplified. When does restricting information flows and constricting control help firms deal with threats, and under what circumstances does it make things worse? We know that establishment status is productive up to some threshold, but we do not know what the threshold is. Similarly, many of the pressures thought to produce escalation may be reversible. In what circumstances might decision-makers (like the oil companies drilling, so far fruitlessly, in Kashagan – see Chapter 9) commit the opposite error to escalation and quit a venture that has almost succeeded?

Contrary to escalation theory, some economists argue that decision-makers should not abandon poorly performing projects too hastily as there may be hidden value in continuing. For example, an entire class of warships is to be refitted. The first refit goes badly. This may seem ominous – a sure sign that the project is destined to become another case of escalation. But this judgment overlooks the learning gleaned from the exercise, which may enable the second refit to proceed more smoothly and the third more smoothly still. There is the reputational argument for persistence to consider. Firms that walk away when the going gets rough may find it harder to win work in the future than firms with a reputation for honouring contracts, come what may. Some economists also doubt whether firms should always abandon successful projects in order to pursue even better ones. They argue that it makes sense to do so only if the prospective gains are really big. The answer to these questions may not be obvious. Ultimately, decision-makers must decide whether they are likely to do better in the end by honouring their sunk costs than by observing conventional accounting theory that says ignore them. An even worse error than erroneous persistence or erroneous abandonment may be 'escalating indecision': that is, projects that drift endlessly. It is better to make the wrong decision than to make no decision.

Another question is whether we should be less ambitious. Causal models that assume outcomes are determined by a small set of variables dominate the decision-sciences literature. By contrast, conflict models assume that outcomes result from a complex interplay between forces that promote change and forces that impede it. These so-called contingency models demonstrate that it is the context that makes or breaks: given "x", then "y". They may explain why, for example, introducing new technology in one firm results in a subtle shift in the balance of power between professional and technical staff, but introducing the same technology in another firm has no effect. In short, it all depends.

A good theory has one more attribute: namely "interesting". An interesting theory is one that denies an old truth, challenging our taken-for-granted world. For example, the economy of a society was thought to determine its religion. Max Weber, a sociologist, asserted the contrary: that religion determines the economy. Another taken-for-granted theory is that leaders determine the fate of their firms. Indeed, where would Royal Bank of Scotland be today without Fred Goodwin, Enron without Ken Lay and Lehman Brothers without Dick Fuld? Even so, social scientists have yet to find a conclusive link between leadership and firm performance. The contrary theory is that leaders are mainly figureheads. In this view, successful leaders become successful by being careful to associate themselves only with successful ventures. Conversely, when things go awry, leaders make handy scapegoats. The anti-hero leadership theory is interesting because it alerts us to the potential importance of decisions made beneath the strategic apex. For instance, it throws the spotlight on the part played by Enron's more junior executives who knew about some of the fault lines, such as the losses hidden in offshore accounts. A theory can be interesting without necessarily being true. The value of interesting is that it prompts us to think again about what we know and believe to be true.

Then there are things for which there are no real theories. For instance, computer-based design and testing are becoming increasingly important as they enable new products and services to be launched faster. Conducting training in a synthetic environment also enables cost saving. But there are limits, as sticky pedals, cracked hulls and stranded taxis testify. We cannot blame designers and planners for expecting too much from their models. It is organisations that keep pushing the boundaries. It should worry us that we cannot accurately predict where the limits of safety lie.

Then there is our reverence for rationality. Rational means logical and common sense. In decision-making it is construed more narrowly as it implies the existence of a "right" answer. Yet the "right" answer can be wrong. For instance, rational analysis of the prospects of entering the aviation industry would have told Richard Branson to forget the idea of Virgin Atlantic. Rational analysis would likewise have told Steve Jobs that eschewing Microsoft operating platforms was sheer folly. If decisions that defy common sense can work out well, what do our theories miss?

An intriguing possibility is that a firm's strategy may have nothing to do with notions of competitive advantage and rational choice. More specifically, a small handful of research studies suggest that leaders' strategic preferences are predictable from formative experiences in childhood and early teens. For example, chief executives who have suffered neglect and/or persecution as children may see joint ventures as a threat because their ingrained experiences have taught them to be suspicious and on their guard. Consequently, they may subject any proposals to form partnerships to intense scrutiny or even reject the idea out of hand. Observers may not be aware of the emotional subtext because the leader's response is typically expressed in rational language, such as "wrong fit', "timing is wrong" and "good idea but wrong candidate".

Similarly, the theory predicts that while decision-makers may recognise the need for change, they may be unable to bring themselves to do what is necessary. The most famous example in business history is Henry Ford. Ford insisted on producing the Model T motor car long after sales figures clearly showed that demand was declining. His managers made strenuous efforts to persuade him that a change of direction was required. Ford listened. He understood the arguments. But he was a perfectionist. As he saw it, he had built the perfect motor car and he could not bear to change it. In other words, firms may end up pursuing economically poor lines of activity not so much because of side-bets or prohibitive exit costs (see Chapter 9), but because the leader's early experiences elicit an archaic response.

A more recent example is Dick Fuld, former chief executive of Lehman Brothers. Early on, Fuld's success owed much to his fiercely independent streak. By June 2008, however, the company was in trouble. Analysts advised Fuld to either raise more capital or merge Lehman Brothers with another bank. Neither suggestion appealed to Fuld because they cut across his independence. Only when the company was tottering did Fuld reconsider. By then it was too late. A leader with a different personality might have decided differently. If a venture holds out the possibility of fulfilling some deeply held wish or dream, the decision-maker may pursue it obsessively – for good or for ill.

We can also infer from this that decision-makers are more likely to succeed if they do what feels right for them. Anyone other than Richard Branson entering the aviation industry might well have failed. Anyone other than Steve Jobs going out on a limb may have failed. Similarly, analysts may doubt Nat Rothschild's foray into oil, gas and mining industries. Yet these ventures may work for him. This leads to the additional lesson: know yourself.

To do what feels right we have to know what feels right. Emotions can be seen as another decision-making filter, a shortcut to knowing what seems right. Another word for it is intuition. Intuition is a popular but elusive subject. Although papers have been published in distinguished academic journals, we know little about intuition. We cannot define it. Nor can we explain how it works. Herbert Simon, an economist and Nobel Prize winner, provoked feminist wrath by suggesting that intuition is rational analysis speeded up. Feminists argued that Simon was trying to align intuition with masculine values. All we can say is that intuition is an insight that may be accurate but cannot be explained logically. Call it feelings of knowing.

From the little that is known about intuition, the most important possibility is that it may not be a transferable skill. To be more precise, when HP's chairman and CEO, Carly Fiorina, was ousted in 2005, it was claimed that she did not have the right type of experience. In other words, Fiorina's intuitive reactions may not have been well-suited to HP. If so, it suggests decision-makers are more likely to be successful if they match their choices to what feels right.

When should decision-makers rely upon rational analysis to make choices? When should they trust their intuition? An important theme of this book is that conviction, "feelings of knowing", may be overconfidence or just wishful thinking. Daft ideas can feel right – until we try to implement them. On the other hand, intuition can be as accurate as the predictions of medieval astronomers.

The best approach may be to note intuitive reactions to an idea first. Then analyse it. Analysis can help to differentiate the more promising ideas from the "no-brainers". Where intuition and analysis both point in the same direction, the choice is obvious. Besides, emotional reactions can change. An idea may leave decision-makers cold to begin with. If objective analysis reveals unsuspected potential, they may warm to it.

Supposing analysis reveals that two or three options are almost equal. How should a decision-maker choose between different options when, objectively, there is little to choose between them? The wisest course of action may be to select the option with the greatest emotional appeal. That emotional reaction is saying something.

Finally, what should decision-makers do if rational analysis and intuition point in opposite directions? That is, if analysis (and expert knowledge) says "no" and intuition strongly says "yes". Let Paul Getty have the last word. Getty recounts how geologists decreed that the Red Beds region of Oklahoma could not contain oil:[2]

To me, the area looked as if it might hide oil. Largely on the basis of a hunch, I decided to see for myself. I began drilling in the Red Beds, struck oil and brought in a vast new production field. I suspect that by relying upon such non-textbook thought processes and taking attendant risks, the biggest fortunes have been made – in oil and other endeavours.

There is always something that we do not know. Yet we should also remember that we invariably know more than we can say.

All decisions involving uncertainty run the risk of failure. Emphatically, this book is not meant to dissuade decision-makers from taking risks, though it does advocate that they should pause for long enough to consider them properly. It contains many lessons. The three most important are:

- think (the most important of the three);
- subtract ego from the equation;
- question the "known knowns", that is, that which you are most sure of.

A thinking checklist

- What might I be getting into?
- What assumptions are being made?
- How realistic are those assumptions?
- What about the "figures behind the figures"?
- What are the opportunity costs?
- Am I hearing what I want to hear?
- What am I not hearing?
- What might have changed?
- How might events play out?
- What am I not expecting?

Notes

Acknowledgements

1 Barbara Windle, *Quaker Faith and Practice: The Book of Christian Discipline of the Yearly Meeting of the Religious Society of Friends (Quakers) in Britain*, 2nd edn, Quaker Books, 1999.

I Illusions of control: the confidence trap

1 Taylor, S.E., *Positive Illusions*, Basic Books, 1980.
2 Frean, A. and Lea, R., "Toyota recall: last words from a family killed as Lexus crashed", *The Times*, February 3rd 2010.
3 "Advices and queries", *Quaker Faith and Practice*, op. cit.

2 Blinkered vision: the judgement trap

1 For a more academic review, see Schwenk, C.R., "Cognitive simplification processes in strategic decision-making", *Strategic Management Journal*, 5, 1984.
2 For access to the various research studies into anchoring and adjustment biases see Bazerman, M.H. and Moore, D.A., *Judgment in Managerial Decision-Making*, Wiley, 2009.
3 Board of Banking Supervision, *Report of the Inquiry into the Circumstances of the Collapse of Barings*, London, HMSO, 1995.
4 For a comprehensive explanation of the dynamics of sense-making see Weick, K.E., *Sense Making in Organizations*, Sage, 1995.
5 Treasury Committee, *Barings Bank and International Regulation: Minutes of Evidence*, London, HMSO, May 15th 1996.
6 Wilson, D.C., Hickson, D.J. and Miller, S., "How organizations can overbalance: decision overreach as a reason for failure", *American Behavioral Scientist*, 39, 1996. The identity of the brewery is unknown.
7 Sorkin, A.R., *Too Big to Fail*, Allen Lane, 2009.
8 *Behind Closed Doors: BCCI: The Biggest Bank Fraud in History*, Financial Times, 1991.

9 Weick, K.E. and Sutcliffe, K.M., *Managing the Unexpected: Assuring High Performance in an Age of Complexity*, Jossey-Bass, 2001.

10 Heraclitus: No man ever steps in the same river twice, for it's not the same river and he's not the same man.

3 Ghosts and shadows: where is reality?

1 *National Commission on the BP Deepwater Horizon Oil Spill and Offshore Drilling*, 2010. References to the Deepwater Horizon disaster and related incidents draw mainly on this highly readable report.

2 Cohen, M.D., March, J.G. and Olsen, J.P., "A garbage can model of organizational choice", *Administrative Science Quarterly*, 17, 1972.

3 Mintzberg, H.A., Raisingham, D. and Thoeret, A., "The structure of un-structured decision processes", *Administrative Science Quarterly*, 21, 1976.

4 Kuhn, T., *The Structure of Scientific Revolutions*, University of Chicago, 1970.

5 Herrigel, E., *Zen in the Art of Archery*, Vintage Books, 1989.

6 Weick, K.E. and Sutcliffe, K.M., *Managing the Unexpected: Assuring High Performance in an Age of Complexity*, Jossey-Bass, 2001.

4 Gorilla in the room: information and decision-making

1 See, for example, Brown, R.H., *A Poetic for Sociology*, Cambridge University Press, 1977.

2 Morgan, G., *Images of Organization*, Sage, 1986.

3 For a good discussion see Weick, K.E., "Cosmos vs. chaos: sense and nonsense in electronic contexts", *Organizational Dynamics*, 14, 1985.

4 Green, M. (ed.), *Knowing and Being: Essays by Michael Polanyi*, Routledge, 1969.

5 Dobbs, M., *One Minute to Midnight: Kennedy, Khrushchev, and Castro on the Brink of Nuclear War*, Arrow, 2009.

6 Bower, T., *The Squeeze: Oil, Money and Greed in the 21st Century*, HarperPress, 2010.

5 Conspiracies of optimism: group dynamics

1 For an engaging discussion of group dynamics see Leavitt, H.J., "Suppose we took groups seriously...", in Staw, B.M. (ed.), *Psychological Dimensions or Organizational Behavior*, Prentice Hall, 1995.

2 For access to the academic literature see Strasser, G., Vaughn, S.I. and Stewart, D.D., "Pooling unshared information: the benefits of knowing how access to information is distributed among group members", *Organizational Behavior and Human Decision Processes*, 82, 2000.

3   Gapper, J. and Denton, N., *All That Glitters*, Penguin, 1996.
4   See, for example, Fraser, C., Gouge, C. and Billig, M., "Risky shifts, cautious shifts and group polarization", *European Journal of Social Psychology*, 50, 1971.
5   Myers, D.G. and Lamm, H., "The group polarization phenomenon", *Psychological Bulletin*, 83, 1976.
6   To access the research literature see Eisenhardt, K., "Making fast strategic decisions in high velocity environments: toward a mid-range theory", *Academy of Management Journal*, 32, 1989.
7   Lewis M., *The Big Short: Inside the Doomsday Machine*, Penguin, 2010.

6   Shifting tides: power and politics in decision-making

1   For a fascinating account of the dynamics of power see Wrong, D.H., *Power, Its Forms, Bases and Uses*, Basil Blackwell, 1979.
2   For an interesting discussion see Brown, R.H., "Bureaucracy as praxis: toward a political phenomenology of formal organizations", *Administrative Science Quarterly*, 23, 1978.
3   Mechanic, D., "Sources of power of lower participants in complex organizations", *Administrative Science Quarterly*, 7, 1962. This is the seminal paper on informal power. The distinction between formal and informal power is of course a simplification. In practice, the edges are often blurred.
4   For advice on how to acquire power informally see Pfeffer, J., *Power, Why Some People Have It and Others Don't*, HarperCollins, 2010.
5   For a good discussion of political tactics in firms see Pfeffer, J., *Power in Organizations*, Pitman, 1981.
6   Guler, I., "Throwing good money after bad? A multi-level study of sequential decision-making in the venture capital industry", *Administrative Science Quarterly*, 52, 2007.
7   Pettigrew, A.M., *The Politics of Decision Making*, Tavistock, 1979.
8   For a useful guide to handling conflict see Ury, W., *Getting Past No: Negotiating With Difficult People*, Century Business, 1991.
9   For more information see De Bono, E., *Parallel Thinking*, Penguin, 1995.
10   Brass, D., "Microsoft's creative destruction", *New York Times*, February 4th 2010. Dick Brass was vice-president at Microsoft from 1997 to 2004.
11   Charles Haddon-Cave, *The Nimrod Review: An Independent Review into the Broader Issues surrounding the loss of RAF Nimrod MR2 Aircraft XV230 in Afghanistan in 2006*, London: The Stationery Office.
12   Kramer, K.R., "Re-visiting the Bay of Pigs and Vietnam decisions 25 years later: how well has the groupthink hypothesis stood the test of time?" *Organizational Behavior and Human Decision Processes*, 73, 1995. Rusk kept quiet about his reservations over what would become the Bay of Pigs fiasco in 1961 (see Chapter 6).

7 Predictable surprises

1 Rickert, E., *Chaucer's World*, Oxford University Press, 1948.
2 Cohen, M.D., March, J.G. and Olsen, J.P., "A garbage can model of organizational choice", *Administrative Science Quarterly*, 17, 1972.
3 Bazerman, M.H. and Samuelson, W.F., "I won the auction but don't want the prize", *Journal of Conflict Resolution*, 27, 1983.
4 Reich, C., "The confessions of Sigmund Warburg", *Institutional Investor*, March 1980, a rare interview shortly before Warburg died. Warburg also mentions the problems of establishment status in this interview.
5 Hardin, G., "The tragedy of the commons", *Science*, 162, 1968.
6 Miller, D., *The Icarus Paradox*, HarperCollins, 1992.
7 Starbuck, W.H., "Keeping a butterfly and elephant in a house of cards: the elements of exceptional success", *Journal of Management Studies*, 30, 1993.
8 Drummond, H., *Escalation of Commitment: The Tragedy of Taurus*, Oxford University Press, 1996.
9 Peters, T.J., "Symbols, patterns and settings: an optimistic case for getting things done", *Organizational Dynamics*, 7, 1978.
10 Zott, C. and Huy, C.N. "How entrepreneurs use symbolic management to acquire resources", *Administrative Science Quarterly*, 52, 2007. The section on fledgling entrepreneurs is drawn from this study. Incidentally, for best results, entrepreneurs should employ a variety of tactics and use them frequently.

8 The march of folly: the escalation trap

1 Fay, S., *Beyond Greed*, Viking, 1982.
2 Fay, op. cit.
3 Drummond, H., *Escalation in Decision-Making: The Tragedy of TAURUS*, Oxford University Press, 1996. The account in this chapter is highly abridged.
4 Drummond, op. cit.
5 This was an experiment with theatre tickets reported in Arkes, H.R. and Blumer, C., "The psychology of sunk costs", *Organisational Behaviour and Human Performance*, 35, 1985.
6 The seminal paper is Kahneman, D. and Tversky, A., "Prospect theory: an analysis of decision under risk", *Econometrica*, 47, 1979. For a more readable account see Kahneman, D. and Tversky, A., "The psychology of preferences", *Scientific American*, 246, 1982.
7 Drummond, op. cit.
8 Northcraft, G. and Wolf, G., "Dollars, sense and sunk costs: a life cycle model of resource allocation decisions", *Academy of Management Review*, 1984.

9 Decisionless decisions: the continuity trap

1 Rubin, J.Z., and Brockner, J., "Factors affecting entrapment in waiting situations: the Rosencrantz and Guildenstern effect", *Journal of Personality and Social Psychology*, 31, 1975.
2 Endlich, L., *Goldman Sachs: The Culture of Success*, Time Warner, 1999.
3 Peters, T., *The Little Big Things: 163 Ways to Pursue Excellence*, HarperBusiness, 2010.

10 Risk a little, gain a lot: options thinking

1 The story of Thales is told by Aristotle.
2 There are two kinds of options, financial options and real options. Financial options have a definite expiry date and strike price. By contrast, real options are much more amorphous and therefore difficult to value. There is also controversy about what genuinely constitutes an option, as some economists argue we are in danger of playing fast and loose with the concept.
3 For an accessible discussion see Janney, J.J. and Dess, G.G, "Can real-options analysis improve decision-making? Promises and pitfalls", *Academy of Management Executive*, 18, 2004.

Closing thoughts

1 Camerer, C.F. and Weber, R.A., "The econometrics and behavioral economics of escalation of commitment: a re-examination of Staw and Hoang's NBA data", *Journal of Economic Behavior and Organization*, 39, 1999. The study was Staw, B.M. and Hoang, H., "Sunk costs in the NBA: why draft order affects playing time", *Administrative Science Quarterly*, 40, 1995.
2 Cited in Adair, J., *100 Greatest Ideas for Smart Decision-Making*, Capstone, 2011.

Index